Modern Local Government

In Touch with the People

Presented to Parliament by the Deputy Prime Minister and
Secretary of State for the Environment, Transport and the Regions
by Command of Her Majesty
July 1998

Cm 4014   £12.50

Department of the Environment, Transport and the Regions
Eland House
Bressenden Place
London SW1E 5DU
Telephone 0171 890 3000
Internet service http://www.detr.gov.uk/

ISBN 010 140 1426

Printed in Great Britain on material containing 75% post-consumer waste and 25% ECF pulp.

CONTENTS
Page

Foreword and Introduction

People everywhere deserve and rightly expect a pleasant and safe environment in which they can live and work. We all want good quality public services, with rising standards in our schools and in our health care. We want local communities where everyone can participate in society, and effective care is available to those who need it.

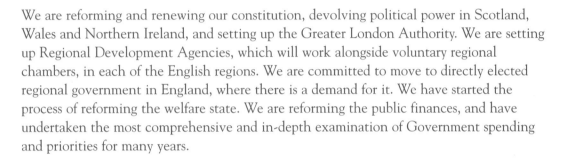

It is to give people this quality of life that we have embarked upon an ambitious programme to modernise Britain. We want to build a fairer more decent society underpinned by stable economic growth, environmental sustainability, and social justice for all.

We are reforming and renewing our constitution, devolving political power in Scotland, Wales and Northern Ireland, and setting up the Greater London Authority. We are setting up Regional Development Agencies, which will work alongside voluntary regional chambers, in each of the English regions. We are committed to move to directly elected regional government in England, where there is a demand for it. We have started the process of reforming the welfare state. We are reforming the public finances, and have undertaken the most comprehensive and in-depth examination of Government spending and priorities for many years.

Central to this programme is our agenda to modernise local government. Among all our public institutions councils have a special status and authority as local, directly-elected bodies. They are uniquely placed to provide vision and leadership to their local communities. They are able to make things happen on the ground – where it really matters.

People need councils which serve them well. Councils need to listen to, lead and build up their local communities. We want to see councils working in partnership with others, making their contribution to the achievement of our aims for improving people's quality of life.

To do this councils need to break free from old fashioned practices and attitudes. There is a long and proud tradition of councils serving their communities. But the world and how we live today is very different from when our current systems of local government were established. There is no future in the old model of councils trying to plan and run most services. It does not provide the services which people want, and cannot do so in today's world. Equally there is no future for councils which are inward looking – more concerned to maintain their structures and protect their vested interests than listening to their local people and leading their communities.

Across the country many councils have already adopted new and imaginative measures. But our modernising agenda is seeking nothing less than a radical refocusing of councils' traditional roles. A fundamental shift of culture throughout local government is essential so that councils become outward looking and responsive. Only in this way will local government fulfil its potential, and councils everywhere contribute to their communities' well-being – that is what people have a right to expect from local democratic institutions.

So we have a demanding agenda for change, which we in central government will take forward in partnership with local government. Over the last six months we have been consulting widely on this agenda. In this White Paper we set out our vision of successfully modernised local government in England, and our strategy for achieving change.

This strategy is to build councils which are in touch with their local people and get the best for them. We will provide a new framework which will give councils the opportunities to modernise and the incentives for them to do so. Every council will need to respond at local level and embrace the change agenda.

The new framework will open the way for councils to adopt new political structures better suited to their role today of community leader – a separation of the executive from councillors' other roles, cabinet systems, executive mayors, including those directly elected. Local democracy will be improved, giving councils opportunities to try out innovative arrangements for local elections, and to consult their local people on key issues through referendums. Crude and universal capping is to be abolished and local financial accountability will be strengthened. A new ethical framework will underpin the standards of conduct of all – councillors and employees – involved in local government.

Within this framework we will want councils to have a duty to promote the economic, social and environmental well-being of their areas. There will be new rules to encourage capital investment. Arrangements for a local business rate supplement will strengthen a council's relationship with its local business community. The more a council demonstrates its capacity for effective community leadership, the greater the range of extra powers which should be available to it to promote the well-being of its area. We will set up a scheme of 'beacon councils' so that the very best councils can be examples to the rest.

There will be a duty on councils to obtain best value in the delivery of local services linked with a rigorous regime of performance indicators and efficiency measures. The thousands of people up and down the land who work hard to deliver good local services deserve appreciation. We are committed to underpin flexibility with fair treatment of well-motivated people and well-trained staff. Councils will need to demonstrate to their communities the quality and efficiency of local services. If a council seriously or persistently fails its community in service delivery, central government will intervene to ensure local people receive the quality of service they need and are entitled to.

This White Paper is but one step along the road of change. Councils are already beginning to embrace the change agenda and to work out at local level what works best for their areas. We want this process to continue and to grow. There is much that every council can do now to modernise.

Once we have established the new framework – and we intend to seek the necessary legislation as Parliamentary time allows – the opportunities for councils to change and modernise will be significantly greater. But it will be for individual councils to work out with their communities how best to use these opportunities.

Only if change comes from within can local government successfully be modernised, able to meet the challenges and needs of the 21st Century. This is the challenge which we in central government and those in local government face today. We will play our part. Every council needs to play its part. If we meet the challenge, the winners will be the people of this country.

JOHN PRESCOTT

SUMMARY

A brief outline of this White Paper

1. This White Paper sets out a strategy for the reform and modernisation of local government in England. It is an agenda for change stretching for ten years or more – well into the 21st century.

Chapter One – the need for change

2. Modern councils should be in touch with the people, provide high quality services and give vision and leadership for local communities. Modern local government plays a vital role in improving the quality of people's lives.

3. Change is needed so that councils everywhere can fulfil this potential. The old culture of paternalism and inwardness needs to be swept away. The framework in which councils operate needs to be renewed.

Chapter Two – bringing about change

4. The Government will introduce legislation to establish this new framework which will provide opportunities and incentives for councils to modernise. The Government will motivate and manage the process of change in partnership with local government. Councils can do much today to reform, and many councils have begun to modernise themselves already.

5. The Government will establish a scheme to select beacon councils to serve as pace-setters and centres of excellence. Councils will be able to seek beacon status for particular services, or for the council as a whole. Those councils which are in touch with local people, have strong and effective links with business, have modern management structures and deliver best value will become beacon councils. Councils with beacon status will get increased scope to act for the benefit of their local community.

Chapter Three – new political structures

6. Councils must have political management structures which are effective and command respect. The current committee system is confusing and inefficient, with significant decisions usually taken elsewhere. Many councillors have little influence over council decisions, yet spend a great deal of their time at council meetings. The result is that people do not know who is running their council.

7. The Government will provide new models of political management for councils. Each model separates the executive role from the backbench role and will provide important and clear roles for all councillors. These models will cover:

- **a directly elected executive mayor with a cabinet.** The mayor will be elected by local people and will appoint a cabinet from among the councillors.

- **a cabinet with a leader.** The leader will be elected by the council, and the cabinet will be made up of councillors either appointed by the leader or elected by the council.

- **a directly elected mayor with a council manager.** The mayor will be elected by local people, with a full time manager appointed by the council.

8. Councils wanting a directly elected mayor will need to obtain popular endorsement through a local referendum. In addition people will be able to petition locally to have a referendum on having a directly elected mayor.

9. Councils will be under a duty to review their political management arrangements and draw up a plan, with a timetable, to introduce one of the new models. The Government will have a reserve power to require councils who drag their feet to hold a referendum on one of the new models. If people reject the proposal, the council will be able to continue with its existing arrangements or propose an alternative model.

Chapter Four – improving local democracy

10. More frequent local elections will strengthen direct accountability to local people by ensuring that voters in every area have greater opportunity to pass judgement on their local representatives. Councils will have a duty to consult local people about plans and services, and will have a power to hold local referendums.

11. The arrangements for local elections are well over 100 years old and need reform to reflect the modern world. There will be new guidance on maximising registration and turnout. Local government will try out ways of making it easier to vote – such as electronic voting, increased postal voting, mobile polling stations and voting on different days.

Chapter Five – improving local financial accountability

12. Strong local financial accountability is important. Crude and universal council tax capping will be ended. Local people will control the spending and taxation decisions of their councils. Councils will be responsible for meeting the council tax benefit costs of high council tax increases. To protect local people, the Government will have a reserve power to control excessive council tax increases.

13. The Government is determined to provide greater stability in council funding. It is therefore announcing the aggregate grant provision for councils for the next three years. The formula for distributing government grant will be stable for the next three years, and there will be a review of the grant allocation system.

Chapter Six – a new ethical framework

14.	There will be a new framework to govern the conduct of councillors and council employees. Councils will be required to adopt a Code of Conduct, based on a national model, which councillors will be under a duty to observe. There will also be a new code of conduct for council employees, built into their conditions of employment.

15.	Councils will have Standards Committees, with at least one independent member, responsible for drawing up the Code of Conduct and advising the council on its implementation and operation.

16.	There will be an independent Standards Board to deal with complaints that councillors have failed to observe the Code of Conduct, with powers to suspend or disqualify councillors. Surcharge will be ended, but there will be powers to recover losses where a councillor or council employee has gained personally at the taxpayer's expense.

Chapter Seven – improving local services through best value

17.	Good local services are vital to people's quality of life. Councils will have a duty to secure best value in the provision of services. The current Compulsory Competitive Tendering (CCT) regime will be abolished.

18.	There will be new national performance indicators for efficiency, cost and quality. Some standards and targets will be set nationally, but in other areas councils will set and publish their own local targets against these indicators.

19.	Councils will be required to undertake fundamental performance reviews of all their services over a five year period, starting with the worst performing. The reviews will:

- **challenge** why and how a service is being provided;

- **compare** the service with the performance that others are achieving;

- **consult** with local taxpayers, service users and the wider business community on how the service can be improved; and

- embrace fair **competition** as a means of securing efficient and effective services.

20.	Councils will prepare annual performance plans, bringing together the outcomes of the fundamental reviews, setting new targets and subsequently reporting back on performance.

21.	There will be new audit and inspection arrangements. External auditors will ensure that local performance plans are accurate and realistic. A new Best Value Inspectorate, working with other Inspectorates, will oversee an objective and independent process of regular inspection of all local services. The Government will act swiftly should councils fail to tackle serious or persistent performance failures.

Chapter Eight – promoting the well-being of communities

22. Effective local leadership is at the heart of modern local government. Councils will have a duty to promote the economic, social and environmental well-being of their area. They will work with other public, private and voluntary organisations and with local people to do this. Councils' powers to work in partnership to tackle cross cutting issues and promote social inclusion will be strengthened.

23. There will be a new legal framework to enable successful councils to do more for their communities and to enable new approaches to public service to be tested through pilots.

Chapter Nine – capital finance

24. The Government is providing extra resources for capital investment in the basic infrastructure of public services. New investment will be for modernisation. The local government capital finance system will be simplified. There will be incentives for councils to make better use of their capital resources and assets.

25. There will be a single capital "pot" so that councils can use resources more flexibly and plan for the long term. Councils will be expected to draw up a comprehensive capital investment strategy. The requirement to set aside for debt repayment receipts from the sales of assets (other than council houses) will be abolished.

Chapter Ten – business rates

26. Councils and local businesses will need to build partnerships to involve business in the council's local tax and spending decisions. The national business rate will be retained. The Government proposes that councils will, within defined limits, be able to set a supplementary local rate, or to give a rebate on the national rate. Beacon councils would be able to vary the rate by a higher percentage, again within an overall limit.

27. Business would not be able to block the setting of a local rate supplement, but the use of any income raised would need to be agreed between the council and local business.

PART ONE

Modernising local government

CHAPTER 1

The need for change

- **Change is needed in local government**

  - **to strengthen the links between councils and local people**

  - **to deliver high standards for local people everywhere**

  - **to spread best practice**

  - **to tackle serious failure**

The modern council

1.1 Councils succeed when they put people first. Successful councils' priorities are to lead their local communities. They organise and support partnerships to develop a vision for their locality, and to contribute to achieving it. They strive for continuous improvement in the delivery of local services. They are committed to best value. They involve and respond to local people and local interests. Their relationship with local businesses and other local organisations is strong and effective. There is trust between them and their local people. It is these councils, in partnership with Government and others, which are able to make real improvements to the quality of people's lives.

1.2 Such councils – modern councils fit for the 21st century – are built on a culture of openness and ready accountability. They have clear and effective political leadership, to catch and retain local people's interest and ensure local accountability. Public participation in debate and decision making is valued, with strategies in place to inform and engage local opinion. Members and employees of the modern council follow the highest standards of conduct.

1.3 To achieve its potential, local government needs the right framework which encourages councils themselves to reform and modernise. Such a framework should promote openness and accountability, provide incentives to councils for improvement and innovation, and produce effective community leadership. The finance system needs to reflect the modern council's relationship with its local community and with central government. And the framework for responding to shortcomings in service delivery, or the conduct of councillors or council employees, must be fair and effective.

Councils today

1.4 This country has a long tradition of democratic local government. So much of what shapes and supports our daily lives is the responsibility of local government. Their responsibilities are central to building a safe, healthy, and pleasant environment in which we live and work. Overall, councils in the United Kingdom spend some £75 billion each year from taxes, around a quarter of all public expenditure.

1.5 Councils can proudly point to their past achievements and the contribution they have made to their cities, towns and villages. And what councils need to do today is just as vital as it was in the past. They are essential to local efforts to raise school standards, house the homeless, care for the elderly, and in partnership with others to planning better health care. Councils have their part to play in regenerating communities, planning transport strategies, and building more prosperous regions through voluntary regional chambers. And it is to their councils that people and communities look when things go wrong – from family breakdown to fire and flood.

1.6 Only some of local government in England today matches up to the picture of the modern council. The current framework in which local government operates has not kept pace with the way people live their lives today. Councils' political structures – centred on the committee system – are fundamentally the same as they were before women had the vote, or indeed, before the introduction of universal male suffrage. The overall framework does not provide the opportunities councils need to modernise, or the incentives for them to do so. Rather the framework is one which allows inefficiencies to continue, and can reinforce a culture where councils are inward looking, failing to put the interests of their people first.

1.7 Although it is right that there is diversity among councils, reflecting differing local priorities and circumstances, people have the right to expect decent quality services wherever they live. Huge variations in service quality, as demonstrated by the Audit Commission's local authority performance indicators, cannot be explained solely by legitimate local diversity. The Audit Commission has concluded that such variations happen largely because of differences in council efficiency.

1.8 Overall, the picture is one where the best councils are excellent, many councils need to drive up their performance standards, and a few councils have failed badly in key local services such as education and personal social services. Such service failures are very damaging for local people, their families, and the local community. Inefficiency and failure are not acceptable and must be tackled.

1.9 So change is needed to drive up standards overall, make best practice more widespread, and address those occasional failures. The aim is not to strangle diversity or create dull uniformity, but to make success universal throughout English local government. This is what the Government wishes to see – strong and effective councils everywhere playing their part in giving people greater opportunities and building a fairer country.

The old culture

1.10 Too often within a council the members and officers take the paternalistic view that it is for them to decide what services are to be provided, on the basis of what suits the council as a service provider. The interests of the public come a poor second best. The culture is still one where more spending and more taxes are seen as the simple solution rather than exploring how to get more out of the available resources.

1.11 In addition where the relationship between a council and its essential local partners – local businesses, voluntary organisations and other public sector bodies – is neither strong nor effective, that council cannot hope to lead its community successfully. Worse, such an inward looking culture can open the door to corruption and wrongdoing.

1.12 Too often local people are indifferent about local democracy, paralleling, and probably reflecting, this culture of inwardness. Over the past years, turnout at local elections has been around 40% and sometimes much less.

Figure 1 Average Turnout in sub-national elections in the European Union	
	% Turnout
Luxembourg*	93
Italy*	85
Belgium*	80
Denmark	80
Germany	72
France	68
Spain	64
Ireland	62
Portugal	60
Netherlands	54
Great Britain	40

* These countries use compulsory voting in at least some areas.

Source: 'Enhancing Local Electoral Turnout – A guide to current practice and future reform' by Rallings, Thrasher and Downe 1996

In the May 1998 local elections the level of turnout on average was even lower. Scarcely more than a third of electors voted in London, compared with a turnout of more than 40% at each of the previous three London borough elections. In other parts of England the turnout reached historic lows. Three metropolitan districts had turnouts of below 20% and there were examples of wards with turnouts of around 10%.

1.13 As a body, councillors do not reflect the make-up of their community – only a quarter are women, only half are employed or self-employed and ethnic minorities are seriously under-represented. There is evidence[1] that councillors – hard working and dedicated as they are – are over burdened, often unproductively, by committee meetings which focus on detail rather than concentrating on the essentials.

1 Representing the People: The Role of Councillors, Audit Commission 1997

The old framework

1.14　This old culture is partly a result of, and is reinforced by, the framework in which local government operates. Much of the way in which the law requires councils to work is straight out of the 19th century (see Annex). But councils face tasks and decisions now which will affect lives in the 21st century. Over recent decades new requirements have been added to this outdated structure, such as Compulsory Competitive Tendering (CCT) and universal capping. This framework of controls has weakened public interest and confidence in local government, and reduced councils' capacity to serve their communities. People and their councils have often been ill-served by such initiatives.

1.15　At the heart of council decision taking and leadership is the committee structure. It is an inefficient and opaque structure for this purpose. It results in councillors spending too many hours on often fruitless meetings – a recent survey showed on average 97 hours per month[2]. It distorts councillors' priorities: 70% of councillors in a recent study[3] felt that representational work directly with the community was their most important role, yet they spent an average of only 30% of their time on it. Above all, the committee system leads to the real decisions being taken elsewhere, behind closed doors, with little open, democratic scrutiny and where many councillors feel unable to influence events. In short, people, businesses, and other organisations in the community do not know who runs their council – who takes the decisions; who to hold to account; who to complain to when things go wrong.

1.16　The framework for local elections is equally outmoded. Although there are strengths in our electoral arrangements – and the United Kingdom has an enviable record of electoral probity – they have failed to keep pace with modern life. The way we cast our vote is the way our great grandfathers voted. The arrangements for registration and for voting do not allow for the mobility of people today. People move area with a frequency not dreamt of when the registration arrangements were established. Where people live, and hence are required to cast their vote, is often not where they work. Apart from elections the formal framework in which councils test public opinion is weak or non-existent.

1.17　Local accountability for levels of council tax needs to be improved. It is weakened by a lack of stability and transparency in Government funding. Crude and universal council tax capping also undermines local accountability, as do the arrangements for council tax benefit subsidy.

1.18　Public confidence in local government is not supported by the current standards regime for the personal conduct of councillors and council employees. As the Nolan Report[4] concluded, there is in local government a profusion of rules resulting in a growing lack of clarity in standards of personal conduct.

1.19　The current framework of powers limits the capacity of councils to lead their communities. The present arrangement for business rates provides a stable, predictable, and simple tax

---

2　Managing Change: Councillors and the New Local Government, Nirmala Rao, Joseph Rowntree Foundation 1992

3　The Local Government Councillor in 1993, Kay Young and N Rao, Joseph Rowntree Foundation/LGC Publications 1994

4　Third Report of the Committee on Standards in Public Life: Standards of Conduct in Local Government in England, Scotland and Wales, July 1997 Cm 3702

for business, which gives a level playing field across the country. But it does not encourage councils to build a strong and effective relationship with local businesses. It detracts from councils' capacity to involve business as a key stakeholder in the local community, and in the decisions which affect their local area.

1.20 On top of this, the current framework for service delivery has proved inflexible in practice, often leading to the demoralisation of those expected to provide quality services and to high staff turnover. Concentration on CCT has neglected service quality and led to uneven and uncertain efficiency gains. In short, this framework has provided a poor deal for local people, for employees, and for employers.

The change agenda

1.21 What needs to be changed is therefore clear. Our aim is that councils everywhere should embrace the new culture of openness and ready accountability. We want to see any culture of indifference about local democracy dispersed, and local people taking a lively interest in their council and its affairs.

1.22 The Government will provide opportunities and incentives for these fundamental shifts of culture by putting in place a renewed framework in which local government in England will operate. This will address the weaknesses and shortcomings in the existing framework, and allow and encourage councils everywhere to modernise. It will open the door to more effective local political leadership, to re-invigorated local democracy, and to quality local services.

1.23 Only if councils whole-heartedly embrace this agenda for change will they be able to meet the needs of local people, businesses and the voluntary sector in their area, and fulfil their potential to lead their communities. It is local government, not central government, which has that vital local day to day relationship with people. Central government can change and modernise, and is doing so. It has undertaken a comprehensive review of all Government spending and priorities; the Better Government programme is setting out an agenda for central and local government to work together. Local government too needs to change and modernise, so that people everywhere can have the quality of life they have the right to expect.

CHAPTER 2

Bringing about change

- **Opportunities and incentives for councils to modernise**

- **Beacon councils to set the pace**

- **Councils to act now**

The process of modernisation

2.1   Modernising local government is an immense task – for Government, for councils, for everyone involved. It is an agenda for essential change. The Government is committed to it.

2.2   The Government will provide opportunities and incentives for change. It will support and motivate change, through legislation where necessary, working in partnership with local government and others including business and professional bodies.

2.3   But if change is to be successful and securely rooted it must be embraced at local level. Each individual council will need to carry through its own modernisation process to suit its own local circumstances. This process will be helped where councils can learn and draw on each others' experiences. The national local government bodies – particularly the Local Government Association (the LGA) – are well placed to play the key role here.

The process so far

2.4   The process of change is already underway. Councils have begun to reform and renew their political management structures. Some councils are adopting new and innovative arrangements – insofar as is possible under current legislation – to give clearer political management. They are taking steps to separate out a political executive within their political structures. These steps are designed to enhance local accountability and increase councils' effectiveness as community leaders. There is a growing diversity – and increasing volume – of participation initiatives in local government[5]. Councils are seeing

---

5   Enhancing Public Participation in Local Government: De Montfort University, University of Strathclyde: DETR 1998

consultation as an integral part of any project plan; some councils have a huge range of options for community involvement; many councils have adopted measures to seek the views of young people in particular.

2.5 There are now also many examples of councils being involved in effective partnerships with businesses, the voluntary sector, and others to enhance their area and the quality of life of people who live and work in it. Some councils are actively developing their role as leaders of local communities. Councils are beginning to pursue best value in service delivery (see Chapter 7). Some 40 councils are working with DETR to pilot best value in England, and many others are developing services on best value lines.

2.6 At national level local government is beginning to embrace the change agenda, and to put in place measures to help individual councils as they begin to modernise. The LGA has established its Democracy Network, and has adopted Five Commitments – probity, community government, high quality public services, renewing local democracy, and modernising local government.

2.7 The Government welcomes this process of self-reform. It wants to see it continue and grow. And the Government is playing its part to promote the change agenda. An essential starting point on which to build the modernisation process is the partnership demonstrated in regular Central Local Partnership Meetings. These meetings – chaired by the Deputy Prime Minister, and bringing together Cabinet Ministers and local government Leaders – are now a firm fixture in the calendar. And to demonstrate its commitment to democratic local government, one of the Government's first acts was to sign the European Charter of Local Self-Government. The Government has now ratified this Charter which binds the United Kingdom from 1 August 1998.

2.8 Earlier in 1998 the Government published a series of six consultation papers on aspects of its proposals for modernising local government. These papers were:

- local democracy and community leadership

- improving local services through best value

- business rates

- improving local financial accountability

- capital finance

- a new ethical framework

2.9 The Government thus initiated a wide ranging debate about local government. Lord Hunt of Tanworth introduced into Parliament a Private Member's Bill designed to enable councils to experiment with their political structures. Although the Bill was well received by local authorities, and there was significant interest in the opportunities it presented for modernisation, it did not complete its passage through Parliament.

2.10   The consultation papers attracted significant interest. There were more than 90,000 'hits' on the DETR Internet site to view the six papers, and over 2,500 formal responses were received. The Government is grateful to everyone who sent in views, and has taken careful account of what was said in developing the proposals in this White Paper.

2.11   There was overwhelming support for the Government's analysis of the condition of local government and the need for modernisation. Inevitably, respondents had different views about how best this modernisation should be achieved.

The future process

2.12   This White Paper is the Government's next step in bringing about change. Drawing on the consultation exercise, it charts the future path of the modernisation agenda for English local government. It sets out a strategy to give:

- **a bigger say for local people** by –

    creating new political structures for councils,

    improving local democracy,

    strengthening local financial accountability,

    establishing a new ethical framework, and

- **a better deal for local people** by –

    improving local services through best value,

    councils promoting the well-being of communities,

    simplifying capital finance,

    introducing some local discretion in business rates.

2.13   The Government wants to see councils everywhere put their local people and communities first. Only with such councils will local people get the best. Councils will:

- adopt new ways of working through **new political structures,**

- both by doing this and more generally **improve local democracy and local accountability**, thereby giving themselves a new democratic legitimacy,

- be subject to new disciplines through the **new ethical framework** and **the duty of best value**, and

- be given **new powers,**

so that they will be able to promote the well-being of communities more effectively and guarantee quality in the delivery of local services.

2.14   Few of these changes will affect parish councils directly though the same underlying principles apply. Such councils are already close to their communities. They are an essential part of the structure of local democracy in our country. Parish councils will continue to play a key role in many of our towns and villages. They have a vital role in helping principal councils keep in touch with the smallest communities in their areas. Parish councils can work in partnership with their principal council to bring government closer to the people, and to establish the decentralised delivery of local government services. It is important therefore that parish councils everywhere embrace the new culture of openness and accountability, putting their local people first.

2.15   The Government's role will be to renew the overall framework in which local government operates. Legislation will be introduced to establish this new framework as Parliamentary time allows. The underlying principles of the new framework will be:

- to give councils all the opportunities they need to modernise, to promote the well-being of their communities, and to guarantee quality local services; and

- to provide effective incentives for councils to embrace the modernisation agenda.

2.16   The Government also has a role in partnership with local government actively to motivate and manage the process of change. This process needs to be accepted and pursued at local level by each individual council. Councils will need to share best practice and help each other develop ideas. There will need to be effective training for all those involved in local government. The Government welcomes the steps which the LGA is now taking to meet these needs, and will be inviting the LGA to join with it in partnership to take forward this vital work.

2.17   The renewed framework will have at its heart powerful incentives for councils to modernise. The more a council modernises, the greater will be its capacity to serve its local community effectively, and the more powers and freedoms it will be given. Opportunities to spend will be tied to results. The Government will also establish a scheme of beacon councils.

Beacon councils

2.18　Beacon councils – the very best performing councils – will set the pace of change and encourage the rest to innovate and to modernise. The Government will establish a scheme to identify and select these beacon councils as recognised centres of expertise and excellence to which others should look.

2.19　Ministers will take decisions on awarding beacon status, in response to applications from councils. There will be an independent advisory panel, with an appropriate mix of academics, business people, local government figures, practitioners and service users. The panel will advise Ministers both on selection criteria and on individual applications.

2.20　Councils will be able to apply for beacon status in relation to particular service areas, or for the council as a whole. It is envisaged that in all but a handful of cases applications will initially relate to particular services. There will therefore be beacon housing councils, beacon education councils, or beacon social service councils. A council which obtains beacon status for a number of its key services will then be well placed to apply for overall beacon status. An overall beacon council will be responsive to its local community, have modern management structures, and a successful best value regime demonstrated by high standards of efficiency and effectiveness.

2.21　The criteria for selection will be as objective and transparent as possible. Selection will need to take account of performance in service delivery against national and local performance targets and performance indicators. It will also need to have regard to inspectorate reports, and auditors' statements on financial management. In their applications councils will be expected to demonstrate that they consistently provide efficient and effective services, and that they have a high level of support from local people and the business community.

2.22　Beacon status will be awarded for a fixed period – perhaps three or five years – after which a council will need to reapply. A council would lose beacon status if, for example, serious service failure was identified during that period.

2.23　A council with beacon status for a particular service will be given wider discretion in the way in which that service is managed and delivered. For example, a council could be given more freedom to make capital investment in its beacon service, subject to the council making a proper analysis of the budgetary implications; controls in secondary legislation on service delivery could be eased for a council's beacon service.

2.24　Where a council has overall beacon status, it could be given not only greater discretion in relation to particular services, but additional powers and freedoms giving it greater scope to act for the benefit of its local people and area. This paper describes three particular initiatives where the Government is proposing to make available such additional powers and freedoms – the new reserve capping powers in Chapter 5, the proposed new powers framework in Chapter 8, and the proposals for a supplementary local business rate in Chapter 10.

2.25　It is essential that the scheme of beacon councils commands confidence and respect throughout local government. Before establishing the scheme the Government will consult widely.

Action now

2.26 Much of the change agenda can be taken forward now. Councils should not wait for legislation before they consider how to make further progress to modernise. Councils can now make progress on:

- **their role as community leaders**. They should review and take steps to strengthen relationships with key public, private and voluntary sector organisations in their area. With them, and in consultation with local people, they should develop a strategy for promoting the economic, social and environmental well-being of their area setting out the strategic priorities for the area and the contribution of each of the key contributors;

- **their local democratic arrangements**, including how best to increase local electoral registration and turnout and how to work more closely with business and local people;

- **their arrangements for securing best value**, by planning a programme of fundamental performance reviews of every service, and developing means of consulting and involving the public in the improvement of service provision and cost;

- **their political management arrangements**, starting to separate the executive from the backbench role and establishing effective arrangements for scrutiny of the executive; and

- **their need for capital investment**, and the development of a programme to make optimum use of assets and the resources available to them.

2.27 The good work which councils, the LGA and others have begun can and must continue. For its part, the Government is committed to doing its utmost to encourage and support local government as it continues to bring about the fundamental shift in culture needed for English local government to serve its people today, and in the next century.

PART TWO

A bigger say for local people

CHAPTER 3

New political structures

- **New leadership for communities**
  - **directly elected executive mayor with a cabinet**
  - **cabinet with a leader**
  - **directly elected mayor with a council manager**

- **Local people to decide on directly elected executive mayors**
- **Important and clear roles for all councillors**

Modernisation and new political structures

3.1   New political structures are fundamental to the modernisation process. The right structures are crucial if councils are to be responsive to their local communities, and are to tap the interest and enthusiasm of local people. Councils need to put in place structures which guarantee openness and accountability, and which are best suited to their roles today of leading communities and securing the efficient delivery of quality local services.

3.2   Councils need new structures which create a clear and well known focus for local leadership. Local people should know who takes decisions, who to hold to account, and who to complain to when things go wrong. And a council's structures must not discourage people from seeking to become involved with their council, in particular as councillors.

3.3   There is no one right political structure. There is today already considerable diversity in councils' political structures, reflecting local choice and circumstances, within the current framework. In future there will be greater diversity as councils innovate and introduce new structures to meet the challenges they face.

Political management structures

WHY CHANGE POLITICAL MANAGEMENT STRUCTURES?

3.4 Traditional committee structures, still used by almost all councils, lead to inefficient and opaque decision making. Significant decisions are, in many councils, taken behind closed doors by political groups or even a small group of key people within the majority group. Consequently, many councillors, even those in the majority group, have little influence over council decisions.

3.5 Councillors also spend too much time in committee meetings which, because the decisions have already effectively been taken, are unproductive. Councillors attend too many council meetings. The evidence is that many wish to spend much more time in direct contact with those they represent. They may have had little say in the decisions taken, but they are required to explain the actions of the council, or their party group, to the people they represent. The emphasis ought to be on bringing the views of their community to bear on the council's decisions, and on scrutinising their performance.

3.6 Equally, there is little clear political leadership. This is not a reflection on the qualities of council leaders. It is caused by the structures in which they work.

3.7 People often do not know who is really taking the decisions. They do not know who to praise, who to blame or who to contact with their problems. People identify most readily with an individual, yet there is rarely any identifiable figure leading the local community.

3.8 This is no basis for modern, effective and responsive local government.

WHAT CAN BE DONE?

3.9 Many councils have taken up the challenge of making their decision-taking structures more efficient and effective. The Government is keen to encourage all councils to shake up and reinvent the way they take decisions.

3.10 Some have taken an axe to the number of committees, the number of councillors involved in each meeting and the number of meetings. This streamlining can reduce councillors' attendance at meetings by 40% or more. This leaves more time for councillors to engage directly with those they represent, conducting consultation exercises or playing a part in local neighbourhood forums, for example.

3.11 Different forms of decentralisation can also open up the decision making process and help local communities identify with those who serve and represent them. They can help make councils easier to understand and easier to access. Both decentralisation and streamlining committee structures can play their part in the Government's general aim of bringing government closer to the people.

SEPARATION OF ROLES

3.12 Both the executive and backbench roles of councillors are vital to the health of local democracy and to effective community leadership. Each role can only be fully effective when it is separated from the other. These roles therefore need to be separated and each given its rightful place and powers.

3.13 The executive role would be to propose the policy framework and implement policies within the agreed framework. The role of backbench councillors would be to represent their constituents, share in the policy and budget decisions of the full council, suggest policy improvements, and scrutinise the executive's policy proposals and their implementation. The precise balance between the roles of the executive and backbench councillors in initiating policies will depend on the detail of the arrangements in place.

3.14 The separation of the executive has advantages in terms of efficiency, transparency, and most importantly, accountability.

- **Efficiency:** A small executive, particularly where individuals have executive powers, can act more quickly, responsively and accurately to meet the needs and aspirations of the community.

- **Transparency:** It will be clear to the public who is responsible for decisions. The scrutiny process will help to clarify the reasons for decisions and the facts and analysis on which policy and actions are based.

- **Accountability:** Increased transparency will enable people to measure the executive's actions against the policies on which it was elected. Councillors will no longer have to accept responsibility for decisions in which they took no part. That should sharpen local political debate and increase interest in elections to the council.

3.15 For these reasons, separation of the executive is common to many systems of local government throughout the world. Those areas of the world whose local government systems remained until recently based on ours, such as New Zealand or the Land of North Rhine-Westphalia in the Federal Republic of Germany, have moved away from it. When the new democracies were emerging in Central and Eastern Europe and South Africa, none chose to emulate the British local government system with its lack of distinction between the executive and the backbench.

3.16 English councils can already take some steps to separate these roles. But there is a limit to what can be achieved under current legislation which generally requires decisions to be taken formally by the full council, officers or politically balanced committees.

New models

3.17 The Government has therefore decided to enable and encourage councils to move permanently to new political management structures, based on this separation of the executive role. The Government will introduce legislation to make a number of options available. However, the Government does not believe that these structures are generally appropriate to parish councils who typically have much more constrained functions and a much smaller membership. The options will include:

- A directly elected mayor with a cabinet;

- A cabinet with a leader; and

- A directly elected mayor and council manager.

3.18 Current arrangements include a statutory requirement for there to be a social services committee and provide for Church representatives and parent governors to be co-opted on to education committees. The Government will ensure that proper provision reflecting the importance of a co-ordinated approach to social services and the high priority it attaches to education will be made in each of these models. There will continue to be Church and parent representatives on any council committees which are concerned with education.

A DIRECTLY ELECTED MAYOR WITH A CABINET

3.19 Under this model (Figure 2) the mayor would be elected by the whole electorate. The mayor once elected would select a cabinet from among the councillors. The cabinet could be drawn from a single party or a coalition. It is likely that these cabinet members would have portfolios for which they would take executive decisions acting alone. The mayor would be the political leader for the community, proposing policy for approval by the council and steering implementation by the cabinet through council officers.

3.20 The chief executive and chief officers would be appointed by the full council in line with current practice. The chief executive would have particular responsibility for ensuring that both executive and backbench councillors received all the facilities and officer support necessary to fulfil their respective roles.

A CABINET WITH A LEADER

3.21 Under this model (Figure 3) a leader would be elected by the council and the cabinet would be made up of councillors, either appointed by the leader or elected by the council. As with a directly elected mayor model, the cabinet could be drawn from a single party or a coalition. The model is very similar to that above except that the leader (sometimes known as an indirectly elected mayor) relies on the support of members of the council rather than the electorate for his or her authority and can be replaced by the council. While the leader could have similar executive powers to a directly elected mayor, in practice the leader's powers are less likely to be very broad as there is no direct mandate from the electorate for the leader's programme.

A DIRECTLY ELECTED MAYOR AND COUNCIL MANAGER

3.22 Under this model (Figure 4) a mayor would be directly elected to give a political lead to an officer or 'manager' to whom both strategic policy and day to day decision making would be delegated. The mayor's role is primarily one of influence, guidance and leadership rather than direct decision taking. Using a private sector analogy, the mayor might resemble a non-executive chairman of a company and the council manager its powerful chief executive.

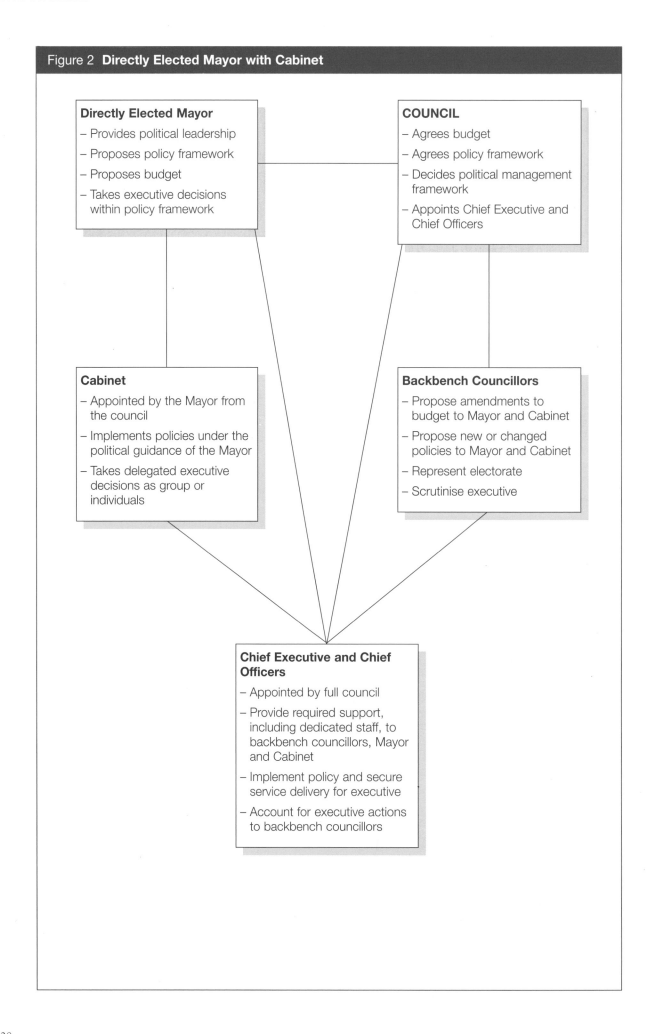

Figure 2 Directly Elected Mayor with Cabinet

Directly Elected Mayor
– Provides political leadership
– Proposes policy framework
– Proposes budget
– Takes executive decisions within policy framework

COUNCIL
– Agrees budget
– Agrees policy framework
– Decides political management framework
– Appoints Chief Executive and Chief Officers

Cabinet
– Appointed by the Mayor from the council
– Implements policies under the political guidance of the Mayor
– Takes delegated executive decisions as group or individuals

Backbench Councillors
– Propose amendments to budget to Mayor and Cabinet
– Propose new or changed policies to Mayor and Cabinet
– Represent electorate
– Scrutinise executive

Chief Executive and Chief Officers
– Appointed by full council
– Provide required support, including dedicated staff, to backbench councillors, Mayor and Cabinet
– Implement policy and secure service delivery for executive
– Account for executive actions to backbench councillors

Figure 3 Cabinet with a Leader

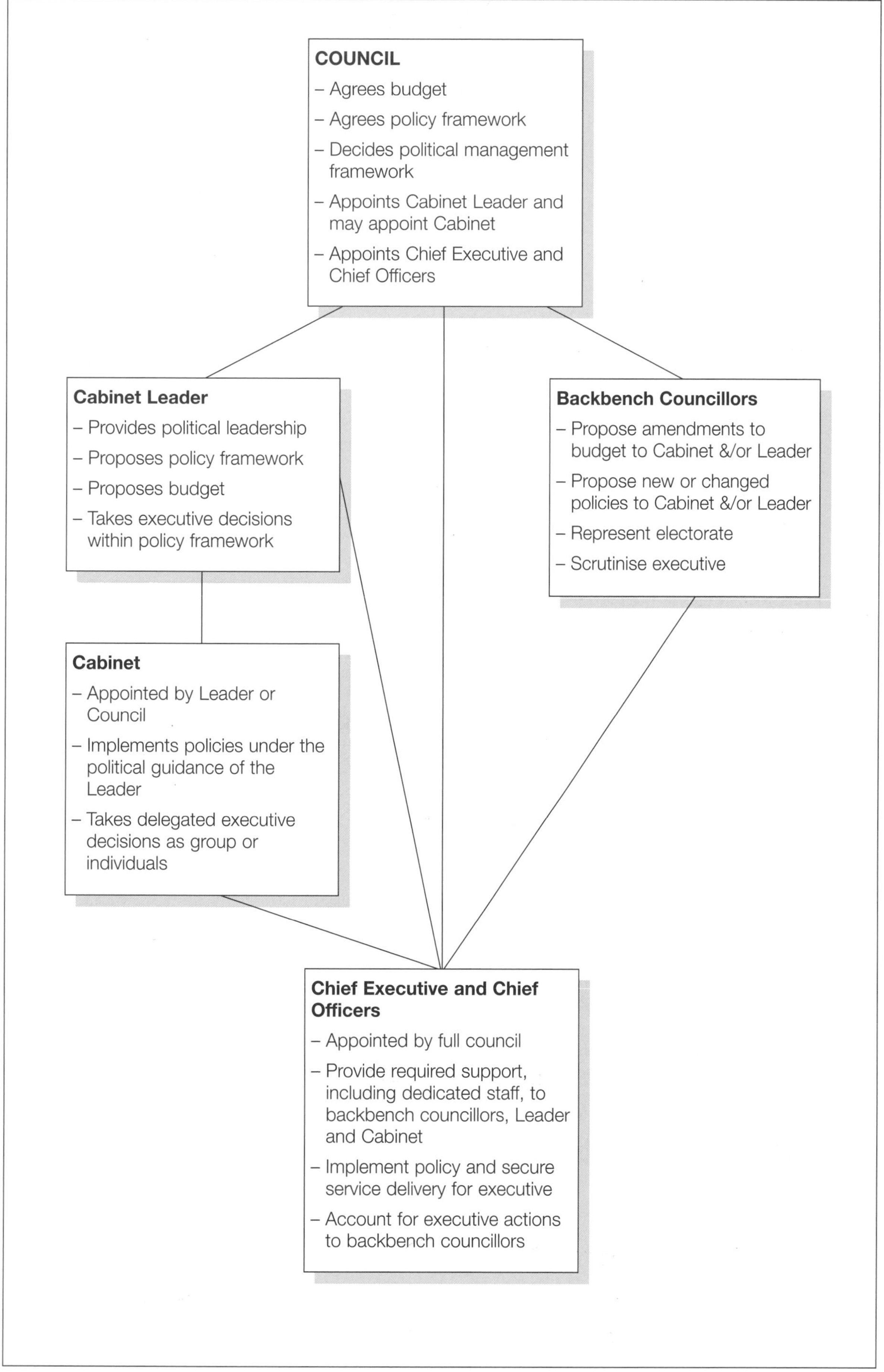

COUNCIL

– Agrees budget

– Agrees policy framework

– Decides political management framework

– Appoints Cabinet Leader and may appoint Cabinet

– Appoints Chief Executive and Chief Officers

Cabinet Leader

– Provides political leadership

– Proposes policy framework

– Proposes budget

– Takes executive decisions within policy framework

Backbench Councillors

– Propose amendments to budget to Cabinet &/or Leader

– Propose new or changed policies to Cabinet &/or Leader

– Represent electorate

– Scrutinise executive

Cabinet

– Appointed by Leader or Council

– Implements policies under the political guidance of the Leader

– Takes delegated executive decisions as group or individuals

Chief Executive and Chief Officers

– Appointed by full council

– Provide required support, including dedicated staff, to backbench councillors, Leader and Cabinet

– Implement policy and secure service delivery for executive

– Account for executive actions to backbench councillors

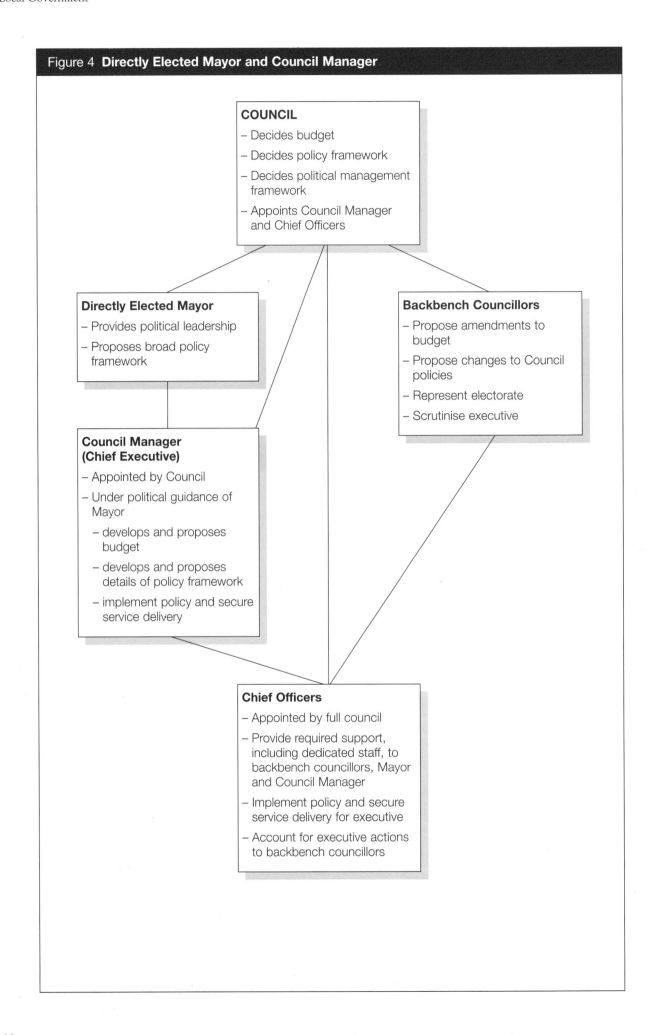

Figure 4 **Directly Elected Mayor and Council Manager**

COUNCIL
- Decides budget
- Decides policy framework
- Decides political management framework
- Appoints Council Manager and Chief Officers

Directly Elected Mayor
- Provides political leadership
- Proposes broad policy framework

Backbench Councillors
- Propose amendments to budget
- Propose changes to Council policies
- Represent electorate
- Scrutinise executive

Council Manager (Chief Executive)
- Appointed by Council
- Under political guidance of Mayor
  - develops and proposes budget
  - develops and proposes details of policy framework
  - implement policy and secure service delivery

Chief Officers
- Appointed by full council
- Provide required support, including dedicated staff, to backbench councillors, Mayor and Council Manager
- Implement policy and secure service delivery for executive
- Account for executive actions to backbench councillors

Choice and diversity

LOCAL CHOICE

3.23 Councils will choose which of these models they prefer and the detail of how they wish to operate within the broad definition of the model. The current and likely political make-up of a council could affect both decisions. For example, different arrangements may appeal to those councils whose ruling groups are coalitions, or where frequent changes of control are likely, to those whose political make-up are more predictable. It is vital that councils have ownership of the processes through which they will take decisions.

3.24 The Government will need to set out key features of these models. They will be based on the recent work produced by a team of expert academics and practitioners led by the Institute of Local Government at the University of Birmingham. The Government will consult widely, including the LGA, the Society of Local Authority Chief Executives and the Audit Commission, before putting any models in place.

3.25 The Government recognises that under any model it will be vital to have clarity about roles, and in particular about where powers to act will reside and the degree of veto or control. It also recognises that placing executive responsibilities upon individuals, as is the case in most of the variants of the proposed models, will not always be appropriate. For example, quasi-judicial functions such as planning, licensing and, perhaps, appeals should not normally be given to individuals. But other decisions are capable of being taken quite properly by an individual subject to scrutiny by other councillors, the local media and the local community and subject to the protection given by the new ethical framework set out in chapter six below.

3.26 The benefits of these new structures are greater the more the executive role is separated and the more direct the link between the executive and the community it serves. The Government is, therefore, attracted to the model of a strong directly elected executive mayor. However, such a figure may not be the right form of political leadership for every council.

ROOM FOR DIVERSITY

3.27 No two councils are run in exactly the same way, yet their political structures are all defined under the single, broad uniform model currently available to them. The scope for diversity, innovation and local choice will be even greater under the Government's proposed new framework than it is under the single model which exists today.

3.28 Not only will local government be more effective and more accountable, but councils everywhere will have greater scope to design a system of governance which is best suited to local circumstances. The Government's proposals will open up a much richer variety of local democratic structures.

3.29 All councils except parishes will be required to prepare proposals for their own decision-taking arrangements, based on these models, and a timetable for their implementation. The Government will provide detailed guidance on the particular issues they need to address. It will be important to safeguard the rights of the public and councillors to information. Freedom of information will apply to these models. The guidance will need to cover these issues as well as the implications for councils' standing orders.

SUPPORT FOR A DIRECTLY ELECTED MAYOR

3.30   In the case of the Greater London Authority, the Government took the view that the people of London should be given the chance to decide, in a referendum, whether or not they supported the creation of a directly elected mayor and separately elected assembly. It believes the same should apply throughout local government. It therefore proposes that before a council could adopt arrangements which include a directly elected mayor it should be required to conduct a referendum on its proposals giving local people the opportunity to have their say.

3.31   In addition, we propose to give local people the right to call for a referendum on whether there should be a directly elected mayor. Such a referendum would be triggered by a petition signed by perhaps 10% of the council's electorate. The result of either form of referendum would be binding.

MAINTAINING MOMENTUM

3.32   The Government believes that all councils should share in the benefits of modern systems of government. But it recognises that councils will need to move at their own pace. Councils will therefore set their own timetable for adopting one of the models set out in this chapter.

3.33   However, the Government proposes to take a reserve power to tackle cases of abuse or inertia. Where a council has developed proposals with a timetable but is failing to act upon them, or has neglected to develop any proposals at all, the Government will have the power to require the council to hold a referendum asking the local electorate to support one of the approved models. The proposition would be set by the Government and might vary between different sorts of authority; different models might be appropriate to rural districts than to urban unitary councils, for example.

3.34   Such referendums would normally be combined with an election for the council. A positive result in the referendum would be binding upon the council. If the electorate voted 'no', the council could continue with their existing arrangements or bring forward alternative proposals.

3.35   In any five year period, there should only be one referendum on the political management structure for a council whether triggered by the Government, council or by petition.

Electing the mayor

3.36   The Government has proposed that the supplementary vote (SV) system should be used for the election of the Mayor for London. The SV system was proposed for London because it is simple and easy to use and can result in a clear winner. In the light of this the Government believes that it may be sensible to adopt similar arrangements for the election of mayors elsewhere.

3.37 Under the SV system voters simply mark the ballot paper using an 'X', as is usual in other elections. The ballot paper has separate columns in which voters may register their first and second choices. Voters are not required to vote twice if they do not wish to do so.

3.38 Counting under the SV system is also simple. Assuming there are more than two candidates, voters' first preferences are counted and if one candidate gets 50% or more of the vote, he or she is elected. If no candidate polls 50% of the vote, all of the candidates are eliminated from the ballot except the two who received the highest number of votes. The second preferences on the ballot papers of the eliminated candidates are then examined and any second votes which have been cast for the remaining candidates are awarded to them. Whoever has the most votes at the end of that process is declared the winner.

The role of the executive

3.39 The role of the executive will be to exercise political leadership on behalf of the council and to represent the area and its community on the wider stage. It would form a clear focus for negotiations with potential partners and others such as the Government, national and international public bodies and businesses considering investing in the council's area.

The responsibilities of the executive will be to:

- translate the wishes of the community into action;

- represent the authority and its community's interests to the outside world;

- build coalitions and work in partnership with all sectors of the community, and bodies from outside the community, including the business and public sectors;

- ensure effective delivery of the programme on which it was elected;

- prepare policy plans and proposals;

- take decisions on resources and priorities; and

- draw up the annual budget, including capital plans, for submission to the full council.

An enhanced role for all councillors

3.40 The separation of the executive role will give all councillors a new enhanced and more rewarding role. Currently, councillors can in practice be excluded from the real decision taking and yet have no power to challenge or scrutinise those decisions.

3.41 Under the new models a council would be required to establish scrutiny committees of backbench councillors. These councillors would be under an explicit duty to review and question the decisions and performance of the executive. They would also review the policies and direction of the council, proposing changes and submitting policy proposals to the executive.

3.42   Backbench councillors will spend less time in council meetings and more time in the local community, at residents' meetings or surgeries. They will be accountable, strong, local representatives for their area. They will bring their constituents' views, concerns and grievances to the council through their council's structures. Their role will be to represent the people to the council rather than to defend the council to the people.

3.43   Each councillor will become a champion of their community defending the public interest in the council and channelling the grievances, needs and aspirations of their electorate into the scrutiny process. In-touch local councillors, aware of and responsive to the needs of those they represent, will have a greater say in the formulation of policy and the solving of local problems than they could have within current committee structures.

3.44   Backbench councillors would also continue to have other important responsibilities vital to the effective functioning of their councils. These would include:

- reviewing and questioning decisions taken by the executive.

- advising the executive on decisions and policy on local issues;

- reviewing policy, formulating policy proposals and submitting proposals to the executive;

- considering the budget proposed by the executive, proposing amendments and voting on the final budget; and

- taking reponsibility, either with or without members of the executive for those quasi-judicial functions, such as planning, licensing and appeals, which it would not normally be appropriate to delegate to an individual member of the executive.

Council officers will support them, or be accountable to them, in all of their roles.

3.45   This enhanced role will provide new opportunities to backbench councillors. The role could be less time-consuming but it will be high profile, involving real and direct responsibilities for the well-being of their community and will be more challenging and rewarding.

The scrutiny role and political balance

3.46   Any arrangement which puts in place a separate executive must include a formal structure for the scrutiny role. That structure must involve all the political parties represented on the council, but its precise form will vary from one council to another. However, it is envisaged that there will be at least one and probably a number of scrutiny committees each taking an overall view of a range of issues.

3.47   The Government believes that the membership of these committees should reflect the political balance between the parties on the council as a whole. Councils will be free to determine the chairmanship of these scrutiny committees as they see fit, but the Government would wish to see arrangements in which opposition parties held some of these posts.

Decentralisation

3.48   Councils have adopted a great variety of decentralised structures for decision taking for a number of reasons. Some have used them to bring together different tiers of local government or to promote coordination between parished areas and non-parished areas. Others have simply created a more local layer of decision taking for their own functions. There is also great variety in the degree of power devolved by different councils under different arrangements.

3.49   The Government supports such approaches to bringing government closer to the people and the diversity of practice that exists. Such arrangements can continue to form a central part of decision making processes under the new models described in this chapter.

3.50   Area committees of councillors could form an important part of any scrutiny structure. They could add a geographical and cross-cutting dimension to the politically balanced and subject based scrutiny at council level. They could be informed by a number of local consultation initiatives varying in their formality.

3.51   An arrangement which delegated executive responsibilities to council officers acting locally under guidance from political representatives or a neighbourhood forum would also be possible under a number of structures. But it may be most appropriate in particular models, such as the elected mayor/council manager model.

3.52   The Government wants all councils to consider carefully how they can bring decision taking closer to the people – to make government easier to access and easier to understand. Decentralisation is a valuable way, but not the only way, of achieving this. The Government will encourage councils to consider, in the course of working up proposals for their future political management structures, whether such arrangements would be desirable in their particular circumstances.

Support for councillors

3.53   A modern council, based on the proposed separation of roles, will rely on the ability of all of its members, whether in the executive or backbench role, to adapt to different ways of working. All councils should give those serving as councillors or as co-opted members the officer support, facilities and training necessary for them to fulfil their role, be it executive or otherwise, as effectively as possible.

3.54   The financial support for councillors must also reinforce the culture of the modern council and address, as far as possible, any disincentives to serving in local politics. People do not enter public service to make their fortune. But neither should they pay a price for serving the public. It is clear that executive mayors, and some others in political executive positions or the scrutiny function in councils, may spend much if not all of their time on council business with a possible subsequent loss of earnings and pension rights. Where this is the case, the Government will make possible the payment of pensionable salaries.

3.55   The level of allowances for councillors is, and will remain, a matter for councils to decide, and for which they are locally accountable. However, the Government will encourage councils to take a radical look at the way in which their remuneration and allowances structures can reinforce the new approach to local government.

3.56   Some councils are already thinking radically about steps to break the attendance culture. A number have done away with attendance allowances altogether. The Government supports this. It wants to see the end of the attendance culture; it therefore proposes to end the attendance allowance.

3.57   The Government will invite the LGA to join with it in drawing up guidance on allowances and the criteria that should be applied in determining what level of allowance should be set. In addition the Government will also require all councils to seek proposals for their allowances and remuneration scheme from a local independent panel. The proposals will be made public but will not be binding; the authority will be free to set allowances and remuneration at a different level to those recommended. But the Government believes that it is important that there is an external public source of advice on what seems an appropriate payment for each of the different roles being performed by members of the council.

3.58   In addition, to address some further disincentives to serve on a council, the Government will confirm the ability of councils to meet the extra childcare or other care costs of their councillors. And it will review current rules on travel and subsistence for councillors and on compensation for loss of earnings for co-optees.

More representative councillors

3.59   The Government's consultation paper on local democracy and community leadership quoted recent research[6] which makes clear that the current body of councillors is not representative of the population as a whole. Fewer councillors are employed, fewer are drawn from the ethnic minorities, many more are over 45 and many fewer are women, than is the case generally. Of course, councillors do their very best to represent their communities, whether or not they share the same background. But the general position cannot be healthy for local democracy.

3.60   The Government wishes to see more councillors drawn from each of these groups in future. In particular, there is a need for more talented, vigorous young people in local government able and willing to make a difference to the world around them. Councils should take all opportunities, particularly in the context of streamlining their structures, to consider how their meetings can be scheduled to accommodate those with jobs or other commitments.

3.61   The Government believes that the combination of the new rewarding roles envisaged for councillors and these steps to address some potential financial and other disincentives to serve will encourage a wider cross section of the community – more employed people, more women, more people from ethnic minorities, more young people and people with young families – to serve their communities in future.

The role of council officers

3.62   Officers will have a crucial part to play in managing the transition to new decision-making arrangements and will continue to play a central role in all councils in these new arrangements. Without a highly effective, imaginative and politically neutral officer

6   The Impact of Releasing People for Council Duties, Social and Community Planning Research, DETR, 1998

service councils will not reap the full potential benefits of these new models. Indeed, this is a pre-condition for a model in which a mayor provides a political steer to a council manager charged with executive delivery of the policy.

3.63   Officers will continue to be given delegated responsibility to take decisions on behalf of the local authority under all of these models. Indeed, there are advantages in extensive delegation of executive decisions and implementation. The political executive will establish their policy and strategy, and drive it through. Backbench members will scrutinise the actions of the executive – both those of the executive's political leadership and those of officers implementing that leadership's policies. The extent of delegation to officers will depend on the precise arrangements a council adopts but, for example, the mayor and council manager model would require considerably more delegation to officers than is currently the norm or would be expected under other models.

3.64   Both councillors and officers will need to adapt to new roles. Officers will continue to service the whole council and support all councillors in their new roles, both members of the executive and those performing the scrutiny role. They will need to provide councillors with the information and facilities they need to be fully effective. They will support councillors in their enhanced role as representatives and leaders of their community, advising on and helping to arrange local consultation on behalf of the executive and local backbench councillors, for example.

3.65   Depending on the precise model a council adopts, within the officer corps some officers may have the specific role of supporting backbench councillors, others supporting the mayor or leader and cabinet. The great majority of employees will carry out the authority's policies and deliver or secure services: They will be responsible to the political executive through their line management with statutory duties to account for their actions to the council in its scrutiny role.

3.66   In all cases there will continue to be a Chief Executive, appointed by the whole council, heading up the whole officer corps. He or she will lead and manage that corps, and ensure that it properly fulfils all its duties to the mayor or leader and all other members of the council in their several roles.

3.67   The benefits of streamlining the political management of the authority should extend to both councillors and council officers. Rather than attending and servicing large numbers of generally unproductive meetings, officers will be able to devote more of their time to the effective management of the council and successful policy implementation, with clear direction from the political leadership. This will be a key factor in the achievement of best value and meeting the needs of local communities.

CHAPTER 4

Improving local democracy

- **Duty on councils to consult local people**

- **More frequent elections**

- **Easier ways of voting**

4.1 New political structures will help councils to engage with their local communities more effectively. Local people will be encouraged to take greater interest in their council's affairs. New structures alone will not bring about renewal of local democracy which is necessary if councils are to be confident that they are reflecting the priorities and wishes of the people they serve. That can only come about if there is higher participation in elections and close and regular contact between a council and local people between elections. This cannot happen if local people are not interested or feel that the council, or their views about it, are irrelevant.

4.2 This cycle is difficult to break, but the onus is on councils to do it; no-one else can. But the Government will establish a framework which will reinforce and encourage local efforts to improve the quality of local democracy in their area. There are three main elements to the framework:

- help for councils to develop their arrangements for participation and consultation;

- more frequent elections; and

- developments in electoral procedures.

Participation

4.3 Local democracy will remain deficient without a clear and close relationship between councillors (both executive and backbench) and their communities. All those involved need to develop their skills and need the right facilities and support to be able to operate fully effectively. But there is also a need to develop and adopt effective tools for engaging with local people. This is equally true of both backbench councillors and those in the executive, including directly elected mayors.

4.4 The Government's consultation paper on local democracy and community leadership described a number of methods councils have used for consulting those they serve. There is also much academic work which has found yet more approaches being used by councils. The most recent example is the Government-sponsored research by De Montfort and Strathclyde Universities.[7]

4.5 This clearly showed that most councils use a number of forms of consultation and that their use is growing. But the growth in the use of traditional methods, such as consultation papers and public meetings, is much slower than the rapid rise in recent years of the more innovative approaches to participation.

DUTY TO CONSULT

4.6 The Government wishes to see consultation and participation embedded into the culture of all councils, including parishes, and undertaken across a wide range of each council's responsibilities. It will be a key feature of the approach to producing a community plan and achieving best value through performance review and the development of local performance plans.

4.7 The Government proposes therefore to legislate for a new statutory duty on councils to consult and engage with their local communities on these issues. Every council will have to decide which methods are the most appropriate in their own particular circumstances. The Government does not propose to specify the form such consultation should take. The way in which a council conducts consultation will be one of the issues taken into account in assessing how far an authority is meeting its duty of best value or is fit to be a beacon council.

REFERENDUMS

4.8 The Government believes that councils should see and use referendums as an important tool to give local people a bigger say. The Government will therefore introduce legislation to confirm the power of councils to hold referendums. However, they would be neither obligatory nor binding except in the particular circumstances described in the previous chapter. Councils might wish to use referendums to consult their local people on such issues as major local developments or matters of particular local controversy.

---

7 Enhancing Public Participation in Local Government, De Montfort University/University of Strathclyde, DETR, 1998

More frequent elections

4.9   The Government's consultation paper on local democracy and community leadership set out options for moving to elections every year for all councils other than parishes. The response was mixed. Some councils felt that voter fatigue might set in if the electorate were called to the polls every year. Others opposed elections every year but continued to support their current system of four year terms for councillors and electing a third of their members in each of three years out of four – commonly known as annual elections.

4.10   In introducing annual accountability, the Government will therefore build on this well-supported system which is already in place in many councils. All the metropolitan district councils elect by thirds in this way, as do a number of the shire unitary district councils and district councils in two-tier areas. The Government will make this the standard pattern of elections for all unitary councils in future, including London Boroughs.

4.11   The 'fallow' year in which there would be no election for councillors would be used for other elections. In unitary councils (including London Boroughs) which had moved to a model with a directly elected mayor, the mayoral election would take place in the fallow year. So would the elections for the mayor and assembly of the Greater London Authority.

4.12   In two tier areas, the Government is equally committed to giving voters an annual opportunity to pass judgement on their local representatives. But it is also preferable to avoid having annual elections for councils in both tiers.

4.13   In these areas, the Government will therefore introduce a pattern in which both the districts and counties would elect by halves in alternate years; i.e. in year one half of the district council would be elected, in year two half of the county council would be elected, and so on. Such a pattern will be readily understood by local electors.

4.14   Currently most district (lower-tier) councils and the biggest spenders, the counties, have elections only every four years while some district councils are elected by thirds. The Government's proposal will therefore reduce the frequency of elections in some district councils but increase the frequency of elections in most councils. Parishes will continue to hold all out elections every four years alongside local district council elections.

4.15   The Local Government Commission (LGC) will continue to review electoral boundaries in the light of the existing criteria of reflecting local communities and providing for effective local government. But local accountability is maximised where the whole electorate in a council's area is involved in elections each time they take place. This requires the same number of councillors in a ward or electoral division as there are elections for the council in any four year period. The Government will therefore take a power to direct the Commission to take this criterion into account when reviewing a council's electoral areas.

4.16   That means that the LGC could, where possible, and over time, be asked to redefine electoral boundaries to increase the proportion of the electorate involved in each local election. But there is no intention to move towards very large electoral areas in sparsely populated rural areas. These would fail to reflect local communities and place additional burdens on those councillors attempting to represent those who elected them. Single member wards or electoral divisions will continue in many authorities.

Innovations in electoral procedures

4.17   The current electoral processes were designed last century and have, in large part, stood the test of time. But we need to look forward to the new millennium – to encourage people to register, to remove disincentives to vote, to make voting easier and to streamline or modernise the process of voting or counting the votes.

4.18   The consultation paper on local democracy and community leadership suggested a number of initiatives which could help achieve these aims. In every case the majority of responses was in favour of at least trying out those suggestions. Well over 80% of respondents on these issues supported early polling and electronic voting, for example. Even more, over 90%, supported a move to rolling registration. The responses also contained many ideas on best practice.

4.19   The Home Office Working Party on Electoral Procedures, including representatives of local government, central government and the political parties, has considered these responses. In the light of the responses and the advice of the Working Party, the Government has concluded that it should work with expert practitioners to consolidate, develop and improve guidance to reflect current best practice on:

- maximising registration;

- encouraging voter participation in elections – particularly among the young;

- improving access for people with disabilities;

- improving the effectiveness of the official poll card; and

- the role of publicity in achieving many of these objectives.

4.20 The Government will also legislate to enable councils to experiment in the way local elections are conducted. Such experiments could include:

- electronic voting;

- mobile polling stations;

- voting at any polling station in the authority, or for example, at specified places in a nearby authority;

- voting in different hours, on different days, or over a number of days;

- entire elections by postal vote;

- changes in the procedures for postal voting; and

- electronic or mechanical counting of votes.

4.21 The Government must safeguard the integrity of elections and ensure that any experiments do not lead to an increase in electoral fraud. Experiments would therefore have to be sanctioned by the Government. In some cases it would work directly with chosen councils to develop the rules for an experiment. In all cases it will be important that potential local voters have full confidence in the change being piloted – for example, electronic voting.

4.22 The Government also consulted on matters which may not be suitable for the pilot approach. In particular it sought views on rolling registration, as under current arrangements too many people can only vote in elections which may be many miles away from their new homes, and for a council from which they no longer receive any services. There was wide support for this and the other matters raised.

4.23 The Government will therefore develop proposals for a move to rolling registration and to allow aids to assist disabled people to vote in polling stations. It will also review other aspects of electoral practice such as anonymous registration (i.e. withholding the names of individuals at risk from the public register), and how absent voting on demand might be introduced.

Voting systems

4.24 As the Government explained in its consultation paper on local democracy and community leadership, the tradition in this country is for there to be a close link between constituency representatives and those they represent. Our local government voting system delivers just this result, with each councillor being elected by the people of the ward or electoral district which he or she represents. Close links between councillors and the people they represent are vital to ensuring councils engage effectively with their local communities.

4.25   This voting system can sometimes result in virtual one-party rule. Some authorities with an overwhelming majority for one party can be extremely effective and responsive to the needs of those they serve. But this situation can also lead to councils becoming complacent and out of touch.

4.26   The Government does not propose to change the local government voting system other than the possible introduction of the supplementary vote for the election of directly elected mayors. It does not view changes to the voting system as a panacea for the current weaknesses in local government. Local government modernisation is more fundamental than simply changing how people cast their vote. The Government favours a wider and more radical reform programme, encompassing electoral arrangements, political management, finance, service provision and consultation as set out in this White Paper.

4.27   However, the Government has established an Independent Commission on Voting Systems, chaired by Lord Jenkins of Hillhead, to recommend an alternative to the first-past-the-post system for elections to the Westminster Parliament. Once this Commission has reported, and the people have decided which alternative they prefer, the Government will wish to assess the implications for local government.

CHAPTER 5

Improving local financial accountability

- **Crude and universal capping abolished**

- **New safeguards for local taxpayers**

- **More stability in council funding**

Local financial accountability

5.1   Strengthening local financial accountability is vital. It is as important as creating new political structures and improving local democracy, if councils everywhere are to put their local people and communities first.

5.2   Strong local financial accountability means that local people can have an impact on their council's spending and taxation decisions. Those decisions need to be open and understandable. Local people need to take responsibility for the consequences of those decisions. And the costs of local services need to be shared fairly between local taxpayers through the council tax.

5.3   Central government of course has a strong interest in local government's taxation and spending decisions. Councils are responsible for around a quarter of public spending, covering a number of key services, such as education and social services. The Government's aims are to ensure the best value for money and the most efficient possible use of resources in the delivery of all public services, while keeping the overall burden of taxation as low as possible. These aims apply equally to local government spending as to other public spending. Moreover, the bulk of local spending is, and will continue to be, financed by the national taxpayer, so there is a very high degree of interconnection between central and local decisions on councils' finances.

5.4   The financial system for local government needs to reflect both the importance of local accountability and the strong interests of central Government. The arrangements in place today are a relatively blunt way of safeguarding the Government's interests. They weaken local accountability, and do not always serve central Government well.

5.5   Improvements are needed. Crude and universal council tax capping, with central Government in effect setting a budget limit for every council, means that local people's impact on their council's spending and taxing decisions is weak. Moreover, the lack of stability in Government funding over past years means that people do not easily know where responsibility lies for changes in the level of their council taxes.

5.6   These weaknesses are compounded by councils too often failing to engage with and involve their local citizens. Too often councils' decision making lacks openness and transparency. The result is a weakening in councils' democratic legitimacy.

Abolition of crude and universal capping

5.7   The new political structures and improvements to local democracy described in the preceding Chapters are designed to give councils a new democratic legitimacy. With these changes councils will have a more robust democratic mandate to set taxes at the levels needed to deliver local services according to local priorities, of a quality and at a price local taxpayers demand and are willing to pay for. Moreover, councils will be subject to the discipline of best value, securing the efficient and effective use of the resources which they raise. The Government will therefore end crude and universal capping. In particular, the Government will not in advance tell every single council in the country how much it may spend.

5.8   This change itself will contribute to a further strengthening of local accountability. With the Government no longer telling each council what it may spend, local people once again will be able to have more impact on their council's spending and taxation decisions.

5.9   Given its own strong interest in local government taxation and spending decisions, the Government must have reserve powers which will enable it to limit excessive council tax increases should circumstances make that necessary. Provided that councils act in a responsible way, the use of these reserve powers will very much be the exception rather than the rule. Should situations arise where a council's budget increase is judged excessive, either because the increase is particularly large or because the council falls short of the standards of efficiency and economy that people rightly expect for their public services, the Government will be able to respond.

5.10 The new legislation will be more discriminating. It will be capable of excluding defined categories of council from the impact of the reserve power. It will prevent inconsistency, and unfair or arbitrary focus on particular councils. It will need to meet the needs of a range of possible circumstances. The reserve power will also need to be capable of application to individual councils, or larger groups of councils if that proves necessary. The aim will be to allow limits to be put into effect earlier in the financial year than has been possible under current legislation.

5.11 The Government, therefore, will seek legislation to repeal the existing capping laws, and to take reserve powers:

- to look at a council's budget increases over a number of years, allowing it to exempt councils which had small increases in earlier years, or to limit the increases of councils which had cumulatively increased by more than a prudent amount;

- to allow councils whose increases were limited to reduce their budgets over a number of years, rather than requiring them to make the full adjustment in one year;

- where necessary, to require councils to reduce their budget requirement to below that in previous years or below their Standard Spending Assessments (SSA);

- to set no limits on increases by councils meeting certain criteria – for example those whose council tax was only a small proportion of the total council tax bill faced by local taxpayers, those with small budgets, those which provide only particular services; and

- to take into account factors such as the council's performance in the delivery of best value, the support of the local electorate for the council's proposed budget and whether the council has beacon status in deciding whether a council's budget increase is considered excessive.

5.12 If the reserve power were to be used, the main intention would be to limit excessive council tax rises. The Government considers that this could be achieved, as in the present arrangements, by legislation which bears on councils' budget requirements.

5.13 In the period prior to new capping legislation coming into effect, the Government will use existing capping powers as a reserve power to limit excessive council tax increases. Capping principles will not be announced in advance but those councils considered to have set excessive budgets would be capped after they had set their budgets. The Government expects councils to act responsibly in this interim period, as well as later.

Stability – SSAs and grant

5.14 Stronger local financial accountability also depends on people understanding better the link between their council's spending decisions and the council tax bills which they face. People need to know easily where responsibility lies for council tax changes. It will be easier for them to see the effect of their council's decisions on their local tax bills, if there is stability year on year in the funding which Government gives to councils.

5.15 Setting out the aggregate levels of central government grant for a period of years, together with an indication of how it would be distributed, will support this objective. It will be necessary to keep these totals under review, for example to reflect changing responsibilities of central or local government or other circumstances which might impact on levels of service provision. The Government has, therefore, announced the aggregate grant provision to councils for the next three years.

5.16 One of the most important elements for determining the distribution of grant is the methodology used for calculating SSAs. The Government is prepared to look again, before the 1999/2000 local government finance settlement, at changes to improve the present SSAs. The impact of any changes would be dealt with in the usual way. But after that central government, in partnership with local government, intends to set a three year programme of research to investigate thoroughly whether there is a better way of determining the distribution of revenue support grant which is simpler, more stable, more robust and fairer than the present arrangements for SSAs.

5.17   While the investigation is taking place, the Government will not expect to make fresh changes to the method of calculation of SSAs, except for example where there are changes in the functions of councils, or the financing of particular services. The SSAs of individual councils will change to reflect changes in demand for their services as reflected in the data used to calculate the SSAs.

Greater responsibility for council tax benefit subsidy

5.18   The Government's interest in councils' taxation and spending decisions is particularly sharply focused in relation to the reimbursement of council tax benefit costs through subsidy. On average a fifth of any increase in council tax is met by the Exchequer through council tax benefit. A council which levies high council taxes should not be able to rely in this way on the national tax payer to pick up the bill in its entirety for the escalating council tax benefit costs resulting from its own decisions. Moreover, the more fully the national tax payer meets such costs, the more obscured is the link between local spending and local taxation.

5.19   The Government will, therefore, set each year a guideline increase in council tax which would be eligible for council tax benefit subsidy, but above which any increase will be partly ineligible. The Government will protect poorer areas by making arrangements so that councils with above average proportions of residents receiving council tax benefit are not affected more severely than a council with an average proportion of residents in receipt of the benefit. None of these changes will affect an individual council tax payer's entitlement to council tax benefit. Council tax payers on benefit will not be penalised.

5.20   At present the billing authority administers council tax benefit and receives the associated subsidy. In order to give a direct link between spending decisions and tax consequences, particularly for upper tier authorities, the Government will develop arrangements to ensure that any reduction in subsidy will be met by council tax payers across the whole of the area of the council which has triggered the subsidy reduction.

Council tax

5.21   The council tax is working well as a local tax. It has been widely accepted and is generally very well understood. This has been borne out by the responses received to the consultation paper.

5.22   While there are always opportunities for improvement, there are no fundamental problems that need urgent attention. The Government has decided that raising standards of council services and making councils more accountable to the people they serve are more pressing priorities, and that any adjustments to council tax should be made at a later date.

5.23   The strength of a property based tax rests on the robustness of the valuation of property on which it is levied. Council tax was designed to avoid the problems of the earlier rates system by placing properties into wide valuation bands. The banding system means that there have to be major changes in relative property prices before significant numbers of households are being unfairly treated. This makes it possible to extend the period between expensive and potentially disruptive revaluations, particularly as the cost of a revaluation is over £100 million.

5.24   The Government has concluded that the current valuation base remains broadly acceptable, and is likely to remain so for the next few years. In these circumstances it does not propose to carry out a revaluation in the course of the current Parliament.

5.25   In time there will be a need for a revaluation, although it is difficult to predict when this will become essential. The Government recognises that a general revaluation gives an opportunity to re-examine the number and width of the property bands, as many council respondents have asked it to do. It will keep the fairness of the system under review, and carry out the first revaluation during the next Parliament if it proves necessary. At that time, and in the light of the experience of council tax since 1992/93, the Government will also consider again whether to bring forward legislation to ensure that regular revaluations are automatically part of the system.

CHAPTER 6

A new ethical framework

- **High standards of conduct for councillors and council employees**

- **Strict codes of conduct**

- **Effective enforcement and disciplinary arrangements**

  - **all councils to have standards committees**

  - **a new independent Standards Board**

  - **end of surcharge**

6.1 The conduct of everyone in local government – councillors and council employees – needs to be of the highest standard. On this depends that bond of trust between councils and their local people which is essential if councils are to play their part in leading communities and improving people's quality of life.

6.2 Where a council embraces the new culture of openness and ready accountability, this will shape the personal conduct of everyone involved. In a council which puts people first, the culture will be one where public service is valued, and where the highest standards of personal conduct are the norm.

6.3 To underpin standards of conduct in local government, the Government will establish a new ethical framework. This framework will be built on the recommendations in the Third Report[8] of the Committee on Standards in Public Life on Standards of Conduct in Local Government ('the Nolan Report'), and on the proposals set out in the consultation paper published earlier this year. It is described in the following paragraphs, which are the Government's formal response to the Nolan Report.

6.4 The Government will introduce legislation which will require every council to adopt a Code of Conduct, which all its members will be obliged to observe. There will be arrangements, supervised by a new Standards Board, for the investigation of all allegations that a council's Code of Conduct has been breached. In England the Standards Board will be a new independent body with a presence in each region. The Government is minded to apply the principles of these arrangements to Police Authorities, taking into account their

8 Third Report of the Committee on Standards in Public Life: Standards of Conduct in Local Government in England, Scotland, and Wales, July 1997 Cm 3702.

special circumstances. There will be separate arrangements in Scotland and Wales. There will also be a new Code of Conduct for council employees, which will form part of their terms and conditions of employment.

New codes of conduct for councillors

6.5   The Government agrees with the recommendation of the Nolan Report that the existing National Code of Local Government Conduct should be replaced. In England, where the structure of local government is more varied than in the completely unitary arrangements in Scotland and Wales, there is widespread support for the view that councils should have some scope to adopt their own codes, adapted to their organisation, structure and functions, including common national principles. Local ownership of standards should make codes more effective.

6.6   Each council's Code will be required to contain General Principles of Conduct which will be common to the Codes of all councils. Each Code will also set out rules of conduct which the council concerned has decided, given its local circumstances, are to apply to the behaviour of its councillors. Councils will be guided by a Model Code as to the rules of conduct which they will be required to include in their Codes and those which they will be able to include or omit according to their circumstances.

THE GENERAL PRINCIPLES OF CONDUCT

6.7   The General Principles should be put to Parliament for approval and it would be mandatory for each local code to include them. Figure 5 shows an illustration of what should be covered, subject to Parliamentary approval. All elected members will have to observe these principles.

Figure 5 General Principles

These principles have been approved by resolution of both Houses of Parliament. Elected councillors of local authorities in England are expected to behave according to the highest standards of personal conduct in the performance of their duties. In particular, elected councillors must observe the following principles of conduct.

Community leadership
You should promote and support these principles by leadership and example, always acting in such a way as to preserve public confidence in the council.

Duty to uphold the law
You have a duty to uphold the law, and to act on all occasions in accordance with the public trust placed in you.

Constituency
You have a duty to assist the council to act as far as possible in the interests of the whole community that it serves. Where constituents' interests are in conflict with those of other groups or areas, you should help to ensure that the council is aware of them and that constituents are able to pursue their concerns, but you are not obliged to put the interests of constituents above the general interest.

Selflessness
You should act solely in the public interest. You should never use your position as a councillor to gain for yourself, your family or your friends any financial benefits, preferential treatment or other advantage, or to confer such benefits, treatment or advantage improperly on others.

Figure 5 (cont.) **General Principles**

Integrity and propriety

You should not put yourself in a position where your integrity is called into question by any financial or other obligation. As well as avoiding actual impropriety, you should avoid any appearance of it.

Hospitality

You should record all gifts and hospitality received in connection with membership of the council. You should not accept gifts or hospitality that might reasonably be thought to influence, or be intended to influence, your judgement; or where to do so could bring discredit upon the council.

Decisions

Whilst you may very properly be influenced by the views of others, including your political group, it is your responsibility to decide what view to take, and how to vote, on any question which councillors have to decide.

Objectivity in decision-taking

In carrying out public business, including making public appointments, awarding contracts, or recommending individuals for rewards and benefits, you should make decisions on merit.

Accountability

You are accountable to the electorate and the council's wider community for your actions and your part in reaching decisions, and must submit yourself to whatever scrutiny is appropriate to your office.

Openness

You should be as open as possible about all your actions and your part in reaching decisions. You should seek to ensure that reasons are given for decisions of your council and that disclosure of information is restricted only in accordance with the law.

Confidentiality

You should also ensure that confidential material, including material about individuals, is handled in accordance with the law and – having regard to the public interest – any decisions on such handling taken by the council; and is not used for private purposes.

Stewardship

You have a responsibility to play your part in ensuring that the council uses its resources prudently and in accordance with the law.

Participation

You may take part in the consideration of questions which come before councillors unless you have a private interest of a kind which, in accordance with this Code, precludes you from participation.

Declarations

You have a duty to declare any private interests relating to your public duties and to take steps to resolve any conflicts arising in a way that protects the public interest. You should make relevant declarations of interest at meetings of the council, its committees and working groups, or any outside body to which you are appointed or nominated by the council, during informal contacts, and meetings of your political party, and in all circumstances where you are active in your role as a councillor.

Relations with officers

You should respect the role of the council's officers and employees and treat them in a way that engenders mutual respect at all times.

RULES OF CONDUCT: THE MODEL CODE

6.8 The General Principles will be incorporated in a Model Code, on which all local codes will be based. The Government will be inviting the LGA to play a leading role in partnership with others in developing the Model Code. It will be subject to approval by the Secretary of State, and endorsed by Parliament. In addition to the general principles of conduct, it will set out rules addressing the following issues:

- councillors' discharge of their representative function;

- councillors' conduct in relation to direct pecuniary and other interests:

- the relationship between councillors and officers; and

- rules governing the claiming of expenses and allowances and the use of council facilities.

6.9 The Government will keep the new arrangements under review as councils adapt to new ways of working, to ensure that they are appropriate to the change of circumstances. Where, for example, there is a directly elected executive mayor a special Model Code may be needed to reflect clearly the separate responsibilities of the Mayor and the Council.

COUNCILLORS' PERSONAL INTERESTS: REGISTRATION, DECLARATION AND WITHDRAWAL

6.10 Central to each council's Code will be rules relating to the treatment of councillors' personal interests. The Nolan Report was critical of the present approach to councillors' interests, and made a number of recommendations for change.

6.11 The approach will follow the subdivision suggested by Nolan into two categories:

- direct pecuniary interests; councillors would have such an interest in a decision if they or their spouses or partners would stand to benefit or lose financially from that decision; and

- all other interests.

This will be reflected in the arrangements for: registration of interests, declarations of interests and withdrawal from meetings.

REGISTRATION OF INTERESTS

6.12 There will be a statutory duty on each council to establish and maintain a public Register of Members' Interests. The Model Code will contain requirements for councillors to provide the necessary information about their interests to the Monitoring Officer, who will keep the register up to date.

6.13 Failure to register pecuniary interests is at present a criminal offence for councillors, but does not attract criminal sanctions elsewhere in the public sector. The non-pecuniary interests which are to be registered may in any case make it less easy to attach criminal consequences to failure to register. The Government therefore proposes to seek the repeal of the criminal offence, and that the consequences of failure to register should be dealt with through the disciplinary framework.

DECLARATION AND WITHDRAWAL

6.14 The Government proposes to replace the existing legislative framework relating to declaration of interests and withdrawal from discussion. In its place, a mandatory element in the Model Code would require that councillors should not participate in the discussion or determination of matters:

- in which they have a direct pecuniary interest, that is they or their spouses or partners would stand to benefit or lose financially from the decision at issue;

- in which they might appear to be at risk of bias by putting private considerations above the public interest (such a risk of bias, for example, might arise if councillors, and those with whom they are connected, are affected by an issue in a way that does not affect the general population); and

- in which they could be seen to be using their position as a councillor to secure preferential treatment or advantage for themselves or those with whom they are connected.

6.15 Connections would include members of a councillor's household, their family and close friends, and any firm, business, company or organisation by whom the councillor is employed or in which they have a significant interest. Where councillors' interest in an organisation relates to public bodies – for example, where councillors are involved as community or local representatives on boards of school governors, local authority companies, or community associations – the interest should not normally disqualify a councillor unless the issue in question particularly affects that body (to achieve this outcome if the councillor holds a remunerated appointment in the public body, a dispensation may be necessary on account of a direct pecuniary interest). In all cases the test is not whether there is a conscious intention of preferential treatment or bias, but how actions might appear to an ordinary member of the public knowing all the facts.

6.16 Any breach of that rule would be a breach of the Council's Code and would therefore be dealt with through the new disciplinary arrangements. Dispensations from the general rule would be exercised by the council itself unless a direct pecuniary interest was involved, in which case it would be exercised by the Standards Board.

6.17 The General Principles of Conduct for councillors, incorporated in the Model Code, will apply to parish councillors in the same way as to other councillors. Every parish council will be required to adopt a Code drawn up by their district council in consultation with them. These arrangements will provide a sound standards framework for parishes, without placing any undue burden on them. The Government will consider how these new codes of conduct might be applied to other bodies such as police authorities, some of which have currently chosen to regulate the conduct of their members using the existing National Code of Local Government Conduct as a basis. Any arrangements for such bodies will need to reflect their particular constitution, membership and basis of accountability.

New enforcement and disciplinary arrangements

6.18 However effective a council's Code may be, it is also necessary to have in place effective disciplinary arrangements to deal with incidents of misconduct.

NEW ENFORCEMENT ARRANGEMENTS
COUNCILS' STANDARDS COMMITTEES

6.19 Every council will be required to establish and maintain a Standards Committee, responsible for:

- advice to the full council on the adoption of a local Code which properly reflects the mandatory elements of the Model Code;

- advice on the discretionary elements of the council's Code; including monitoring and updating;

- advice on effective implementation of the Code, including the training of councillors in matters of conduct, and advice to individual councillors on such issues as the treatment of personal interests, and on conduct matters more generally;

- the arrangements for councillors to receive dispensations to speak on, or participate in, matters in which they have interests;

- determing apprporiate action on matters referred to it by the Regional Standards Board.

The Government proposes that the Standards Committee should have as full members one or two independent persons selected by the council from a regional list maintained by the independent Standards Board. The Committee would support and be supported by the council's Monitoring Officer, reinforcing his or her informal role of helping to keep up standards of conduct by encouragement, advice and persuasion.

NEW DISCIPLINARY ARRANGEMENTS

6.20 The Government has considered whether the internal Standards Committee, reinforced by its independent Member or Members, should be able to impose new disciplinary sanctions including suspension from the council or disqualification from holding office. The Nolan Committee recommended that Standards Committees should have disciplinary powers, subject to a right of appeal to an independent tribunal by the councillor who had been disciplined.

6.21 Although there was some support for this proposal, many who responded to the consultation had doubts that it would be seen to be effective. The public might tend to see the council as likely to protect its own councillors. Without a wider right of appeal by those who were concerned that justice had not been done, there would be no way of challenging leniency or weakness in dealing with misconduct. There could be a risk of disciplinary procedures being abused to hold up business or change the political balance of the council or its committees, or otherwise misused for factional ends subject to an appeal to the Standards Board.

6.22 The sanctions of suspension from the council and disqualification are serious matters, which might be regarded as determining civil rights, and a fair and open external process is essential. However, a properly constituted internal Standards Committee should be able to reprimand councillors, subject to an appeal to the Standards Board.

THE STANDARDS BOARD

6.23 The Standards Board will be an independent body with a regional structure. All written complaints that a councillor has failed to observe their council's Code will be referred to the regional office of the Board. These complaints might come from the public, councillors or from the Monitoring Officer. The office will need to have arrangements to sift such complaints, and to decide which merit further investigation. It will need to ensure that investigation is thorough, effective and timely. The Standards Board will be as streamlined a body as possible, and there will need to be proper separation between its investigative and adjudicative functions. On receipt of an allegation, the officer responsible in the regional office will have several options, depending on the adequacy of the factual information accompanying the complaint, and the seriousness of the alleged misconduct:

- to refer back to the council, asking for a report from the Monitoring Officer on the facts;

- to pass the complaint to the police, the auditor or the ombudsman if it appears to raise matters of criminality, irregularity or impropriety, or maladministration leading to injustice;

- to commission an external investigation;

- either immediately, or in the light of further investigation, to refer back to the council, recommending that the Standards Committee takes its own action; and

- where the evidence merited it, to proceed to adjudication at which the facts would be put to the councillor who was the subject of the complaint, and disciplinary action determined in the light of a public hearing; in accordance with principles of natural justice, the councillor would have a right to respond, to be represented, and to put his or her case; the case would be heard by a regional panel of the Standards Board, the composition of which would normally reflect a combination of experience of local government, and legal or judicial experience; the panel would be able to impose the sanctions described in paragraph 6.26.

The process is displayed in Figure 6.

6.24 In addition to its role in handling specific cases, the Standards Board will have a proactive role in issuing to councils guidance and information about best practice on issues of conduct. It will support the training tasks of councils' Standards Committees. The Standards Board will maintain regional lists of independent persons available to be co-opted by councils into their Standards Committees.

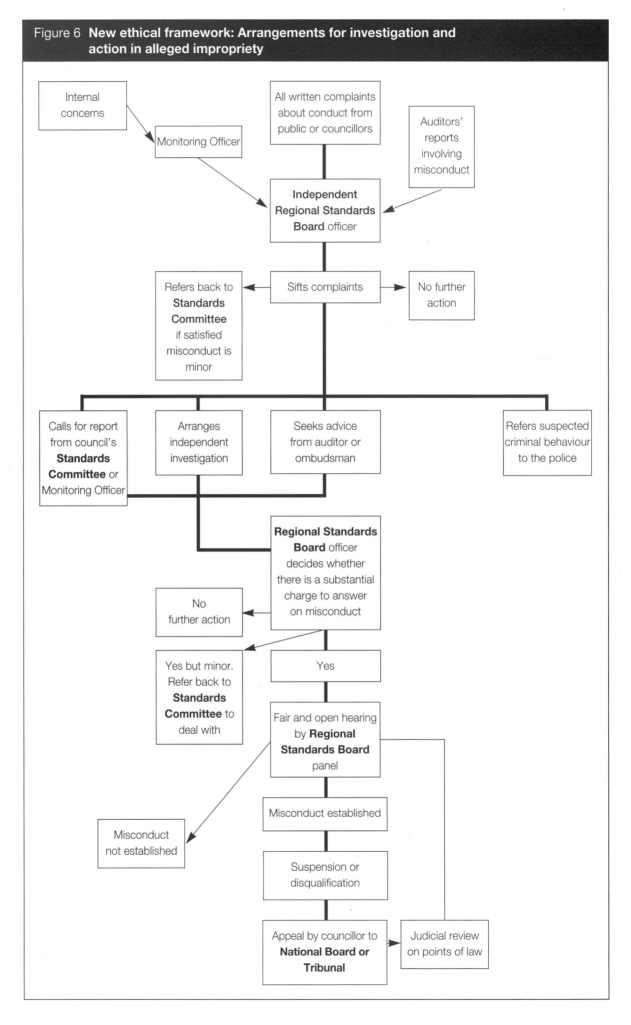

Figure 6 **New ethical framework: Arrangements for investigation and action in alleged impropriety**

6.25   The arrangements for appointment to the Board and for its finance will need to reflect the requirement for the Board to remain independent and to command respect. The Government proposes that the core costs of the Board will be met directly by central government, with the costs of handling particular cases met, subject to further consultation with the LGA, either by recovering costs from the councils concerned, or through a top slice of revenue support grant.

PENALTIES OPEN TO A STANDARDS BOARD REGIONAL PANEL

6.26   The Regional Panels of the Standards Board will be able to impose penalties ranging from public censure, through to suspension from committees or from the council (up to a prescribed maximum period, provisionally three months), up to disqualification from the office of councillor, again up to a maximum period (provisionally five years, the maximum period of disqualification under the audit surcharge regime).

APPEAL AGAINST DECISIONS OF A STANDARDS BOARD REGIONAL PANEL

6.27   The right of appeal will be confined to the councillor who has been disciplined. There is no case for others to be able to appeal against the findings of Standards Boards, although they will be open to judicial review. The Standards Board will be wholly independent and impartial, and therefore there is no need for third party appeals. Appeals by councillors will be heard by a national body. The Government is discussing with the Council on Tribunals whether this will take the form of a Tribunal, or a national panel of the Standards Board itself.

6.28   The appeal body will be able to substitute its own findings for those of the regional panel of the Standards Board, and revise or quash any disciplinary action imposed. As with the Regional Panel of the Standards Board, the National Appeal body will be subject to judicial review.

PARISH COUNCILS

6.29   The requirement to establish a Standards Committee will not extend to parish councils, given their size and limited resources. The maintenance of high standards of conduct are as vital in parish councils as in all other councils. The remit of the Standards Board will therefore cover conduct of parish councillors. The Government wishes to consider with the National Association of Local Councils and the LGA any role a district council might play in strengthening and enforcing standards of conduct in parish councils.

Other enforcement and disciplinary processes

6.30   Both the new arrangements and existing processes – the audit regime and the local Ombudsman – will operate within the wider context of the criminal justice system. In the criminal justice system the Government is considering a number of developments – in particular the reform of the criminal law of corruption and a proposed new statutory offence of misuse of public office – which will have particular significance as regards the interaction of the criminal law and all the local government disciplinary and enforcement processes.

6.31   In working up the arrangements for the Standards Boards, the Government will consult further on their relationship to the functions of the local Ombudsman, the auditor and the police and Director of Public Prosecutions. The aim should be to have clear arrangements, which sort complaints as quickly as possible so that they are pursued through the appropriate channel. The separation of functions will be influenced by the precise formulation of the proposed offence of misuse of public office, and the modernisation of the criminal law on corruption.

6.32   Where complaints are not initially presented as matters of criminality or misconduct, there may be scope for a single clearing house, so that the local ombudsmen, for example, could be approached by a member of the public on any matter, and would undertake to refer complaints to the most appropriate channel for investigation. There will inevitably be complaints where the precise nature of misconduct complained of is not initially clear, and arrangements should be flexible enough to cope with emerging evidence. There will also be instances where both the Standards Board and the Ombudsman or auditor have a role, for example when a complaint alleges misconduct linked to financial irregularity or impropriety, or where misconduct by a councillor leads to maladministration and injustice.

6.33   Further discussion and liaison will be needed to clarify the sequence of events in such cases. For example it may be that the Ombudsman's investigation of whether injustice has arisen from impropriety (eg: a planning application determined by a Committee on which a councillor who should have withdrawn played a part) should follow determination of the misconduct issue by the Standards Board. On matters of financial irregularity, the auditor may be best placed to establish the facts. In general concurrent investigations (with the attendant risk of conflicting findings and double jeopardy) should be avoided.

THE LOCAL OMBUDSMAN REGIME

6.34   The local Ombudsman function will continue to be to address complaints from individuals alleging injustice as a result of a council's maladministration. Since, under the new disciplinary arrangements described above, the primary role in defining standards of conduct will fall to the Standards Board, we accept the Nolan Report's recommendation that the local Ombudsman should cease to issue general guidance about conflicts of interest. As proposed in the consultation paper, to avoid duplication of functions the Government will also seek legislation so that the local Ombudsman will no longer be responsible for taking action against (ie naming) any councillor failing to observe the Code. Disciplinary issues relating to the conduct of individual councillors will be for the Standards Board.

SURCHARGE

6.35   The Government agrees with the Nolan Committee and the majority of respondents to consultation that provision for surcharge of councillors and officers whose wilful misconduct has led to financial loss to the council is archaic and should be repealed. Restitution of financial loss should remain a possibility, but only where the councillor or council employee has gained personally at the expense of the taxpayer, when a compensation order should be available as a means of restoring ill-gotten gains to the Council.

LOCAL GOVERNMENT AUDIT REGIME

6.36   The Government believes that all these developments, perhaps in particular the introduction of the new disciplinary arrangements, will have implications for the audit regime. The Nolan Report recommended that the District Auditor's 'stop' power in England and Wales should be discontinued and replaced by a system of warning notices, and that the right of a local elector to challenge a council's accounts should be recast to avoid abuse of the process. The Government agrees with these recommendations and will take them forward when a legislative opportunity arises.

6.37   The recast right to challenge will take the form of:

- a power for auditors to refuse, for good reasons, to hear objections (subject to a right of appeal) if, for example, they consider the objection vexatious or identical to one previously dealt with:

- a limit on the period of time within which objections can be raised; and

- a simpler and faster process, possibly doing without oral hearings; the auditor might be empowered to set time limits for submission of evidence; it might also be possible to avoid the complexity of the present process in which the objector acts as prosecutor.

The conduct of council staff

THE EMPLOYEES' CODE

6.38   The Government believes that a statutory duty on councils to adopt an Employees' Code will be an important part of the new ethical framework. As with the Code for Councillors, the model for the Employees' Code could be a document prepared by the LGA, in consultation with others, approved by the Secretary of State and endorsed by Parliament. The requirements of the Employees' Code will be included in their terms and conditions of employment. Enforcement of the Employees' Code will therefore be through the staff disciplinary arrangements and employment law.

6.39   The Employees' Code will also incorporate the existing rules governing the political activities of certain local government officers. The Government believes that these rules are necessary for an effective system of democracy and to maintain public confidence. We will however take steps, through an increase in the salary threshold at which posts are assumed to be 'politically restricted', to target the rules more effectively.

THE STATUTORY OFFICERS

6.40   The enforcement and disciplinary arrangements described above place important responsibilities on Monitoring Officers. They endorse the informal role that Monitoring Officers already play in keeping up standards of conduct by encouragement and persuasion, and they also establish a more formal role in the handling of allegations of councillors' breaches of their council's Code. Although, under these arrangements, a Monitoring Officer will not be required to initiate disciplinary action, he or she will be expected to take a view whether an allegation appears to constitute a breach of the Code and, if so, to inform the relevant regional office of the Standards Board. Decisions on the handling of complaints against councillors will need to command respect both within the council and in the wider community. The Government has considered whether to make it a requirement for Monitoring Officer posts to be established at Chief Officer level, and whether the independence of the Monitoring Officer should be strengthened by introducing an explicit requirement that he or she should not also be the Head of Paid Service, but concluded that decisions on these issues are best taken by councils themselves in the light of their own structures and circumstances.

PROTECTION AGAINST DISMISSAL

6.41   Under existing regulations, councils wishing to dismiss a Head of Paid Service on grounds of misconduct must appoint an independent assessor and secure his agreement to their proposed action. The Nolan Report recognises the case for extending this protection to the Monitoring Officer and the Chief Financial Officer. Since Monitoring Officers have a key role in the enforcement and disciplinary arrangements proposed above, there is a strong case for extending protection to them. Chief Financial Officers already play a key role in handling financial propriety issues, including advising members on the lawfulness of proposed expenditure. The external procedures for determination of complaints concerning alleged misconduct of councillors will reinforce the position of the Monitoring Officer who confronts misconduct within the Council, and Chief Finance Officers who confront financial irregularity. The Government therefore accepts the recommendation in the Nolan Report that Monitoring Officers and Chief Financial Officers should have the same protection against dismissal as Heads of Paid Service. The opportunity will be taken to provide that the Regional Standards Board should have a role in appointing the Independent Assessor whose agreement is required before dismissal can be confirmed.

WHISTLEBLOWING

6.42   The Government regards openness as a key element of the process of rebuilding trust between councils and their communities, and accepts the Nolan Report's recommendation that there should be an established procedure for whistleblowing. In developing that procedure, we will draw upon the work of the Local Government Management Board, which has already made recommendations on whistleblowing procedures.

PLANNING

6.43   The Government's preliminary response to the Nolan Report's planning recommendations was set out in Annex C to the consultation paper. This has been widely welcomed, and the Government is pleased to learn of the work already under way in many councils to provide councillor training and to draw up local planning codes. Where substantive comments have been made in relation to particular recommendations, the Government will be taking these into account in its Modernising Planning Initiative.

6.44   The Government has given further consideration to the suggestion that councils should in all cases explain in writing why planning permission has been granted, in contrast to the legal requirement only to give reasons when planning permission is refused, and is taking steps so that when significant development proposals are granted planning permission, the reasons for those decisions are transparent and publicly recorded.

PART THREE

A better deal for local people

CHAPTER 7

Improving local services through best value

- **Councils to deliver best value for local people**

  - **clear service standards**

  - **targets for continuous improvement**

  - **more say for service users**

  - **independent audit and inspection**

- **New powers to act on service failures**

Introduction

7.1 A modern council – or authority – which puts people first will seek to provide services which bear comparison with the best. Not just with the best that other authorities provide but with the best that is on offer from both the public and private sectors. Continuous improvements in both the quality and cost of services will therefore be the hallmark of a modern council, and the test of best value.

7.2 Best value will be a duty to deliver services to clear standards – covering both cost and quality – by the most effective, economic and efficient means available. In carrying out this duty local authorities will be accountable to local people and have a responsibility to central government in its role as representative of the broader national interest. Local authorities will set those standards – covering both cost and quality – for all the services for which they are responsible. But in those areas such as education and social services where the Government has key responsibilities and commitments, the Government itself will set national standards. Here authorities will need to take the national dimension into account in setting their own standards. Under best value local people will be clear about the standards of services which they can expect to receive, and better able to hold their councils to account for their record in meeting them.

7.3   Best value will also help councils to address the cross cutting issues facing their citizens and communities, such as community safety or sustainable development, which are beyond the reach of a single service or service provider. These issues can only be tackled successfully with cooperation between partners and a shared understanding of the outcomes that need to be achieved. The community leadership role proposed for local councils gives them an opportunity to shape the agenda across the board, so that efforts are focused and combined effectively. One of the most significant causes of failure to achieve a best value service is the lack of consideration of how resources are used in relation to common objectives. Best value will support improved performance measurement when council services need to be integrated with those delivered by other public or private agencies and service providers. Whatever the shared aim – it might be to reduce social exclusion, raise standards of public health, or improve air quality – the best value process will help councils decide on priorities in consultation with their communities and other partners, build consensus on what needs to be achieved, and measure how their own programmes and services are contributing to the shared objective.

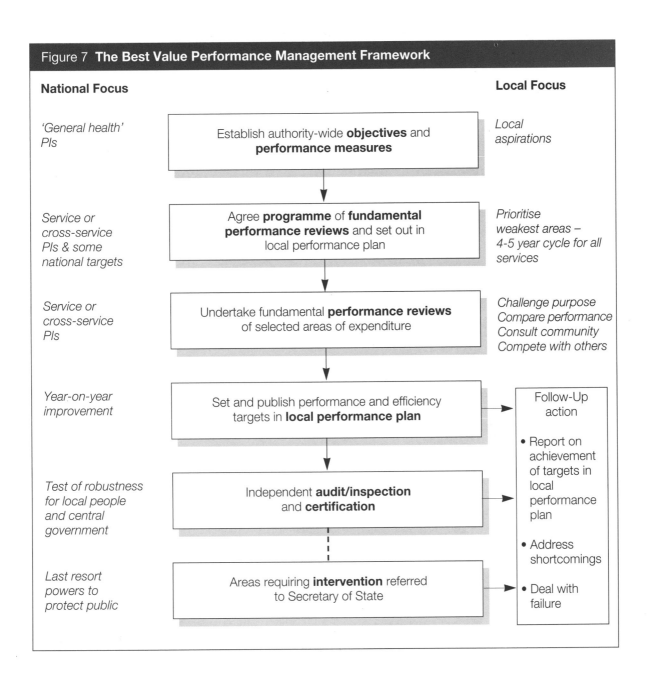

Figure 7 The Best Value Performance Management Framework

National Focus

Local Focus

National Focus		Local Focus
'General health' PIs	Establish authority-wide **objectives** and **performance measures**	Local aspirations
Service or cross-service PIs & some national targets	Agree **programme** of **fundamental performance reviews** and set out in local performance plan	Prioritise weakest areas – 4-5 year cycle for all services
Service or cross-service PIs	Undertake fundamental **performance reviews** of selected areas of expenditure	Challenge purpose Compare performance Consult community Compete with others
Year-on-year improvement	Set and publish performance and efficiency targets in **local performance plan**	Follow-Up action
Test of robustness for local people and central government	Independent **audit/inspection** and **certification**	• Report on achievement of targets in local performance plan
Last resort powers to protect public	Areas requiring **intervention** referred to Secretary of State	• Address shortcomings • Deal with failure

7.4   Our consultation paper 'Improving local services through best value' explained how the Government would make this a reality. There will be a legislative framework which will require authorities to undertake a number of key steps: these are reproduced at Figure 7. The Government accepts that the details of this framework need to be shaped by the experience of local government on the ground. It is encouraged by the enthusiastic start which has been made by the pilot best value authorities and by many others working in partnership to develop a framework with which they identify.

Duty of best value

7.5   We will apply the duty to obtain best value to all authorities that have tax raising or precepting powers, including the proposed Greater London Authority and its constituent parts, and to those with levying powers such as combined fire authorities. The duty will apply to all the services which an authority provides, whether directly or indirectly, and to all the resources at its disposal. The Government recognises, however, that a statutory duty could be onerous if applied in full to the smaller town and parish councils. It will therefore set a de minimis level linked to the limit on financial reporting – probably £500,000 per annum budgeted income – as suggested by the LGA.

7.6   The Government wishes to see best value principles applied to all those working with local authorities whether in partnership or alongside them, and in practice the duty on councils needs to reflect the wider community dimensions. We are taking steps to make this a reality – for example, for central government departments and agencies through the publication of 'Better Quality Services'[9] in the National Health Service, and in the way in which the Housing Corporation exercises its role in respect of registered social landlords. We have consulted closely with the private sector and trade unions. And we accept that local performance plans, for example, will need to demonstrate that proposals for local services flow from a shared vision and focus on key issues. We are not, however, persuaded that a statutory duty of best value should be placed on other public bodies or on private firms at this stage. The Government is considering how best to apply best value to waste disposal services as set out in 'Less Waste: More Value'.[10]

7.7   The Government is not persuaded that a new statutory duty should be placed on the governors of local education authority schools at the present time. But it recognises that the resources provided to schools under delegated budgets are substantial and local people need to be assured that they are obtaining best value from this expenditure. New measures whereby individual schools set targets for improvement, which are subsequently reflected in education development plans approved by the Secretary of State, are to be introduced in the autumn, and schools are rigorously inspected at regular intervals. The Government will explore how efficiency considerations can be built into the model funding scheme for local education authority schools. It also proposes to strengthen the way in which efficiency is built into the regular OFSTED inspections. And it will review the way in which school expenditure is audited to increase transparency and accountability, as both local people and central government need to be sure that they are obtaining best value from this expenditure.

9   Better Quality Services: A handbook on creating public/private partnerships through market testing and contracting out, ISBN 0116309644

10 Less Waste: More Value: Consultation Paper on the Waste Strategy for England and Wales, DETR, 1998

Corporate objectives and performance measures

7.8   Delivering local services to a consistently high standard at an acceptable cost begins with a council's vision for the local community. The council needs to be clear about the services which local people expect and the resources and opportunities available to deliver them. Most authorities recognise that providing everything themselves is both unrealistic and unnecessary. Nor can they achieve all that they want to do in a single year or even in several years. They need to establish priorities and to set them out clearly. These priorities will flow from engagement with the wider community, and from an authority's performance as an organisation and as a provider of services. It needs to know how its work relates to other service providers. It needs to know what local people think of its performance, and what others are capable of achieving, and it needs to know where improvements are most needed. To help authorities establish authority-wide objectives and performance measures, the Government will introduce a new framework of performance indicators, standards and targets.

Performance indicators, standards and targets

PERFORMANCE INDICATORS

7.9   The most effective authorities have long taken steps to satisfy themselves that they know where they stand on the range of services which they provide and where they want to get to. They have developed their own key performance indicators and made constructive use of those which are specified each year by the Audit Commission. The Government will build on that experience to ensure that all councils are able as a start to measure themselves against each other on a variety of key national performance measures.

7.10   This new set of national performance indicators will be developed in consultation with the Audit Commission, with local government and with others. It will include a small number of council-wide 'general health' indicators that will reflect the underlying capacity and performance of local authorities as both democratic institutions and bodies responsible for managing a significant share of public expenditure. For each of the major services there will be key indicators reflecting the effectiveness and quality of local services. Each authority will be expected to set targets in respect of these indicators and to publish both their targets and subsequent performance against them in annual local performance plans. These indicators will be set by the Government itself rather than by the Audit Commission, who will nevertheless continue to have an important role in validating and publishing comparative information, and in supplementing it where it judges appropriate after consultation.

7.11   As far as possible, the indicators will be designed to focus attention on what services have delivered (outcomes), rather than what resources have been devoted to them (inputs). They will enable effective comparisons to be made between the performance of different authorities each year and over time. It will be important to have this performance framework in place as quickly as possible, so that authorities are able to report on performance and set new targets from the outset as soon as best value is introduced. There will be consultation this year on new indicators that could be introduced as early as 1999/2000.

Figure 8 **Paying Housing Benefit and Council Tax Benefit**	
ASPECT OF PERFORMANCE	**INDICATORS**
Strategic Objectives	To ensure x % of those eligible for housing benefit/council tax benefit receive full entitlement
Cost & Efficiency	Administration cost per claimant Percentage of new claims processed within 14 days
Effectiveness	Benefits overpaid as a percentage of total benefit expenditure Percentage of renewal claims for rent allowance processed without a break in service
Quality	The percentage of claimants who said benefits staff were helpful Percentage of new Housing Benefit claims processed within 14 days where the correct benefit entitlement was calculated
Fair Access	The percentage of claimants surveyed who said the claim form was easy to understand

7.12 These indicators – and an example is given for housing benefit and council tax benefit in Figure 8 – will provide a basis upon which authorities can compare performance on a common basis. They will also reflect the national interest in local performance. But in practice most indicators will be developed locally, giving expression to legitimate local differences and aspirations. As such, they will provide a wider context within which performance can be assessed. They will also provide a focus for local debate on essentially local issues. Establishing indicators for local performance is designed to introduce rigour, consistency and transparency, not a straitjacket.

PERFORMANCE STANDARDS

7.13 The Government will provide a clear lead in relation to performance standards where it judges the national interest requires it. An example is the new standards for educational attainment for different age groups, against which authorities will be expected to report performance in education development plans.

PERFORMANCE TARGETS

7.14 Locally set targets in respect of strategic objectives, efficiency, effectiveness, quality and fair access in respect of all key services should be underpinned by a minimum requirement for improvement. The Government will consider how this is best done in the light of new opportunities for change which are emerging in the different service areas. For example, efficiency targets might reflect the substantial efficiency improvement opportunities that IT developments and pooled service delivery provide on services such as council tax collection and benefits administration. Initially, however, the Government will require that as a minimum local authorities set:

- quality targets over five years that, as a minimum, are consistent with the performance of the top 25% of all authorities at the time the targets are set;

- cost and efficiency targets over five years that, as a minimum, are consistent with the performance of the top 25% of authorities in the region at the time the targets are set; and

- annual targets that are demonstrably consistent with the five year targets.

This framework of targets will put most pressure on those authorities who are currently performing poorly on both the quality and the efficiency with which they deliver services. However, it is likely to exert pressure on nearly all authorities because very few authorities score very highly on both aspects of performance at the same time.

7.15   Local government's approach to performance indicators, and the determination with which they carry through service and management reforms which the indicators show to be necessary, will determine how far the framework makes a difference on the ground. The intention, however, is to secure sustained economies from all authorities, as well as continuous improvements in service quality. Local discretion about priorities will be maintained, and an appropriate benchmark will be set against which local people, auditors and inspectors will be able to judge whether or not authorities are obtaining best value. That judgement should be a rounded one, balancing performance across a range of indicators, and taking into account local circumstances.

Fundamental performance reviews

7.16   Authorities will be required at an early stage to assess their priorities and draw up a programme of fundamental performance reviews. They can and should make a start now.

7.17   The Government will require authorities to review fundamentally the performance of all their services over a five year period, making early inroads into areas of significant weakness. Where the performance of a service is demonstrably poor by any standards – and the framework of national indicators will highlight these – then authorities will be expected to review that service quickly and effectively. Where performance is poor but there are a number of areas needing attention, there may need to be some scope for phasing a review. There will also be a case for addressing some of the stronger areas of performance early, so that the lessons of success can be spread quickly. But it would be unacceptable for any authority to put off reviewing significant areas of weakness without good cause; that would be unlikely to find favour with the local community, risk congestion in later years, and itself constitute a failure to achieve best value.

7.18   The purpose of the reviews is to ensure that continuous improvements to all services are made, not just to those where there are serious shortcomings. The principal outcome of each review will therefore be performance targets which take account of national requirements for the service(s) concerned – covering strategic objectives, cost and efficiency, effectiveness, quality and fair access – and an action plan demonstrating how those targets are to be achieved. Each authority will need to explain why the targets have been set as they have, and why they had chosen a particular route to achieve them. In practice, the reviews will:

- **challenge** why and how a service is being provided;

- invite **comparison** with others' performance across a range of relevant indicators, taking into account the views of both service users and potential suppliers;

- **consult** with local taxpayers, service users and the wider business community in the setting of new performance targets; and

- embrace fair **competition** as a means of securing efficient and effective services.

The Government will provide statutory guidance covering all four elements of the reviews.

CHALLENGE

7.19   For each review to be effective in assuring local people that best value is to be obtained, authorities will need to address key questions about the justification for a service and the way in which it is provided. The needs of the public or users of services may change. Such a challenge is also important in that it opens up the possibility of meeting community needs in entirely new ways. New technology or best practice may mean that traditional ways of providing a service are no longer viable or acceptable, and lessons should be drawn from a wide variety of sources. The Government will play its part by seeking to widen the range of options available to authorities through partnerships.

COMPARE

7.20   Authorities will be expected to compare their performance with the best using the national performance indicators and any other means which have been developed locally, for example through benchmarking clubs. Comparison should go beyond local authorities to embrace the experience of other public and voluntary bodies and the private sector. Experience outside local government clearly needs to be interpreted carefully, but there is limited value in comparing performance only against similar organisations with similar perspectives.

CONSULT

7.21   Effective authorities will consult and engage with their local communities in carrying out their reviews. The Government will not prescribe when and how that should be done. Different forms of consultation are needed for the different services and at different stages, and there are existing statutory requirements in some areas. The Government will provide guidance about whether or not statutory consultation rights apply. The right to consultation, such as that afforded to the tenants of local authority housing, has helped give people a real say in the services that directly affect them. The Government will continue to consider the case for such statutory rights on their merits.

COMPETITION

7.22 The Government is committed to building a competitive economy with a flexible labour market, underpinned by the fair treatment of those affected. Local government needs to play its part by securing the real efficiency gains that benefit the nation as a whole, and competition in the broadest sense will help to achieve this. By the same token, real competition is not delivered through the imposition of rules which invite avoidance rather than ownership. CCT made the costs of services more transparent. But its detailed prescription of the form and timing of competition led to unimaginative tendering, and often frustrated rather than enhanced real competition.

7.23 An approach based on partnership rather than confrontation is much better. Competition undertaken in a climate where employees' basic rights are respected and where those employed in delivering services, whether in the private or public sectors, are involved is less threatening but just as challenging. The Government views competition therefore not as an end in itself, but as a means of bringing about the continuous improvements that customers expect and best value demands.

7.24 Well-motivated and well-trained employees are vital in the provision of best value services, whether they are working for local councils, the private sector, or the voluntary sector. The Government wants in future to see employees fully involved in improving the services that they provide to the community. The Government's best value framework aims to build mutual respect and trust, and to bolster confidence in local services. The task of local government will be to combine reassurance to employees with the necessary flexibility to allow transfer on a fair basis to other employers where this is in the public interest.

7.25 Real progress has been made in securing fairness in the labour market for example:

- in establishing minimum standards for all employees through the proposed national minimum wage;

- through the provisions of the Fairness at Work White Paper;[11]

- through the implementation of the Working Time and Young Workers Directives;

- through significant changes to the Acquired Rights Directive which ensure that the legislation is applied more consistently to local government contracting out and partnership deals.

The Government will also review the Transfer of Undertakings (TUPE) regulations in the light of these changes with a view to securing greater certainty in protecting terms and conditions of employment where work is transferred. And it is actively considering with its social partners in industry and the trade unions how pensions, in particular, can be properly protected if work transfers to another contractor, including through admitted bodies status.

7.26 Good procurement practice is essential if local government is to obtain real improvements to service cost and quality. This does not mean a single means of procurement or a single form of service delivery. The Government recognises the benefits that can flow from a dialogue between public, private and voluntary sectors on how to achieve the services that

11 Fairness at Work White Paper, Cm1998

local communities require. Giving effect to this through real partnerships has implications for the way in which services are procured, managed and monitored, as well as for propriety and regularity. The Government will address these issues in Europe and at home, and it will create a climate where partnerships flourish. That is why it will continue to look for ways of modernising the procurement provisions in Part II of the Local Government Act 1988 in consultation with employers and trade unions. The Government will look for an early legislative opportunity to amend the list of factors which authorities can take into account in inviting tenders and awarding contracts, consistent with its European obligations and with the principle of the achievement of value for money.

7.27   These measures will create a more positive climate in which local authorities and their potential partners in the private and voluntary sectors can approach competition – competition which is designed to secure improvements in quality as well as in cost, and is fair to all sides. The key strategic choice for authorities is whether to provide services directly themselves or to secure them through other means. The key test is which of the options is more likely to secure best value for local people. Services should not be delivered directly if other more efficient and effective means are available. The Government will issue guidance which will explain the factors that should be considered in making such a choice.

7.28   The guidance will emphasise that retaining work in-house without subjecting it to real competitive pressure can rarely be justified. Should an authority exercise that choice and the service fail to provide best value, continuing in-house provision would not be sustainable. The guidance will encourage the use of new and innovative forms of partnership. The Government will ensure that appropriate powers are available to provide services to others, and to participate in companies, whilst providing safeguards for local taxpayers. The guidance will also include provision for transparency and robust cost apportionment in accounting practice to ensure that options are assessed on an equal footing and that the role and contribution of trading to best value is clear. In addition, the Government will continue to take firm and swift action against any authority that provides a service to itself, or to others, at a trading loss. Where authorities have incurred significant or sustained deficits on providing services directly, the Government will not hesitate to use its powers to instruct a council to make alternative provision for its services.

7.29   A requirement to use and develop competition as an essential management tool should not be interpreted as a requirement to put everything out to tender. There are a number of ways that an authority might meet the test of competitiveness. It could, for example:

- commission an independent benchmarking report so that it could restructure the in-house service to match the performance of the best private and public sector providers;

- provide a core service in-house and buy in top-up support from the private sector. This would enable comparisons to be made that could help improve in-house performance or result in more of the service being bought-in externally;

- contract out a service to the private sector after a competition between external bidders only;

- form a joint venture or partnership following a competition for an external partner;

- tender part of a service with an in-house team bidding against private sector and other local authority bidders, before deciding whether to provide the bulk of a service internally or externally;

- dispose or sell-off competitively a service and its assets to another provider.

7.30   In the Government's view, the new framework will create the conditions under which there is likely to be greater interest from the private and voluntary sectors in working with local government to deliver quality services at a competitive price. That interest is reflected in the number of networks between private companies and authorities which have developed over the last year, and which the Government is keen to encourage. Participants in these networks have made it clear that they wish to work alongside each other on a constructive basis, with the private sector contributing in a variety of different ways to bring about competitive pressure – whether it is through advice, ideas, tendering, joint ventures or capital investment. The Government will take these developments into account in framing its guidance on competition and the factors to consider in making a strategic choice between the different options.

Local performance plans

7.31   New performance targets will flow from each review. These will be brought together with other service targets in annual local performance plans. Such plans will provide a clear practical expression of an authority's performance in delivering local services and its proposals to improve. In particular the plans will:

- report on current performance, including a comparison with the performance of other authorities;

- identify forward targets for all services on an annual and longer term basis; and

- comment on the means to achieve plans, including proposals for major capital projects and investments, and for the procedural and purchasing changes designed to improve performance.

7.32   Local performance plans will need to reflect authorities' corporate objectives, including those of sustainable development and equal opportunities. And they will complement the various planning and performance management systems already in place or proposed for the key service areas. These planning systems, designed to strengthen transparency and accountability, and in some cases linked to resource allocations from central government, will provide the vehicles through which targets are often delivered.

7.33   Local performance plans will bring together the outcomes from these different planning systems and show authorities' corporate strategy across the range of their responsibilities. These plans will also enable authorities to show how their own plans link with those of other public and community agencies where there is shared responsibility to meet the needs of local people (for example Health Improvement Programmes to deliver the objectives of 'Our Healthier Nation'[12]). They will provide a firm basis for linking local authority plans with those of other public services, like the National Health Service, and with partnership initiatives tackling specific local problems, such as Youth Offending Teams.

12 Our Healthier Nation: a contract for Health, February 1998, Cm3852

7.34 Local authorities need maximum flexibility as to how they present and publish key performance information. The experience of corporate planning initiatives, and that of the current statutory indicators, does not suggest that a single model suits all authorities for all purposes. We will not impose unnecessary uniformity. But the information brought together in the local performance plan will need to be in such a form as to enable broad comparisons to be made between plans year-on-year and between different authorities. Reporting back on performance against targets on a regular basis is essential if local people are to be in a position to judge whether best value has been obtained. Local performance plans will therefore be published within two months of the end of the financial year.

Audit and inspection

7.35 New audit and inspection arrangements will be needed to give a clear view of whether best value is being obtained. There will be a rigorous external check on the information provided by authorities in local performance plans, and on the management systems that underpin them. There will be regular external inspections of performance analogous to those currently being carried out by the separately constituted Inspectorates, such as OFSTED and the Social Services Inspectorate. These arrangements will be consistent with the Government's determination to establish high standards of probity in local government and to restore local accountability. They will be the foundation upon which decisive action will be taken should authorities fail to act when performance falls short. The Government will also ensure that, following consideration by the Public Audit Forum, the new audit arrangements have the capacity to respond to the needs of joined-up government.

7.36 The Government will invite the Audit Commission to draft guidance to local authorities on an internal system of control and audit which would strengthen their capacity for self-assessment. It also welcomes the LGA's proposal to develop a model of self-assessment, based on the Business Excellence Model, which will add to this capacity. This is consistent with the Government's own review of the different quality assurance schemes and it will work with local government to ensure a measure of consistency across the public sector. This, and other quality schemes such as Investors in People, ISO 9000 and the recently relaunched CharterMark, have an important role to play in helping authorities achieve the cultural changes that are needed under best value.

7.37 External auditors will continue to have an important role year on year. They will provide a check on whether:

- the performance and resource information in local performance plans is accurate;

- the plans have been drawn up, and targets set, in accordance with the statutory requirements;

- plans are realistic, having regard to the resources available to the authority.

7.38 The Audit Commission intends to provide guidance to external auditors on the form such checks might take and on the work which might be needed to underpin them. The Government welcomes this, and the steps that have been taken by the Commission and

District Audit to review the skills and resources needed to undertake this work. Resources will need to be managed carefully as these new audit tasks are absorbed. The Government has no plans to change the current system under which such annual audits are funded from the fees paid by local authorities themselves.

7.39   However rigorous the annual process of reporting on performance, it is unrealistic to expect such audits always to provide the in-depth scrutiny of performance that best value requires. The Government attaches great importance to an objective and independent process of regular inspection for all local services. It has already announced its intention to form a new housing inspectorate within the Audit Commission, as part of a new Best Value Inspectorate. This Inspectorate will build on the joint working which the Commission has established with the Social Services Inspectorate and others in recent years, and apply these same principles to all those areas of local government activity not covered by the existing specialist inspectorates.

7.40   The Government will strengthen the interests of service users in local service provision through consultation and their wider involvement. The new Inspectorate will therefore include lay representation as well as specialists selected for the purpose. The Government will consult with the Audit Commission, the LGA and others on how best that representation might be defined and operated in practice.

7.41   The new Inspectorate will be given powers, in common with the specialist inspectorates, to trigger swift and energetic action where an authority's performance falls short of reasonable expectations. It will need to acquire the core skills and expertise to enable it to do so. It will need to develop the capacity to carry out regular inspections of different intensity depending on the service and the performance of the authority concerned. The existing specialist inspectorates will need to adapt in a similar way as best value develops and as an authority's capacity for self assessment improves. They will continue to undertake inspection and other activities in support of Ministers, as well as inspection functions in the best value framework.

7.42   The inspections will confirm that:

●   the fundamental performance reviews have been carried out by authorities in accordance with the legislation and statutory guidance; and

●   the performance targets that have been set for future years are sufficiently challenging to ensure that best value will be obtained for local people.

7.43   Inspection will be designed wherever possible to avoid duplicating the work that authorities have undertaken in their internal reviews. It will not seek to substitute a new set of targets for those set by an authority, but will require authorities to review their targets urgently if that is what is needed. It will be for elected councillors to agree the new targets required, and take responsibility for achieving them.

7.44   The Government will ensure that the different inspectorates work together to ensure a consistent perspective and approach, and avoid timetabling difficulties. It will establish an Inspectorate Forum to discuss common inspection interests, but is not persuaded of the need for a formal lead role to be assigned to any one body to co-ordinate the inspection function under best value. It will keep this under review, however, and will take a power to enable the Secretary of State to make such arrangements as necessary in consultation with the inspectorates to ensure the smooth and efficient operation of the inspection process.

7.45　The Government has also considered how the new Best Value Inspectorate might be funded. It has concluded that the Inspectorate should be partly funded by fee income and partly through grant to the Commission in respect of that function, and will discuss with the Commission the conditions under which such support is given to ensure that the independence of the Commission is not compromised.

Intervention

7.46　The Government will act wherever authorities fail to remedy clear performance failure, either in respect of substance (for example, a shortfall in relation to significant targets or standards) or process (for example, where procedures prescribed as necessary to best value were not followed).

7.47　The Government will introduce legislation to take new powers to support flexible and constructive intervention, and these powers will be available to the appropriate Secretary of State who will be required to consult relevant parties where intervention is proposed. These powers will offer a range of responses. As appropriate to the circumstances, the Secretary of State would be able to require, for example:

- an authority to draw up an action plan for improvement, and deliver a specified level of improvement by a set date;

- an authority to accept external management help;

- services to be put out to competition;

- services to cease to be provided directly by a local authority;

- responsibility to be transferred to another authority or third party in the case of serious service failure.

7.48　The Government will exercise these powers wherever there is serious or persistent failure in the delivery of services. An urgent need for intervention could arise, for example, where vulnerable groups of the population are affected and an authority is unwilling or unable to act sufficiently quickly to protect them. The Government will act on the basis of objective triggers that an authority has failed to achieve best value, or has failed to deliver acceptable standards of service, or has failed to take opportunities to reduce costs and increase quality. The Government accepts, however, that local accountability is best served by authorities themselves acting quickly and effectively to prevent poor performance and to tackle it where it occurs. It welcomes the LGA's proposals to establish a new national improvement agency designed to improve services across the board and to reduce the need for intervention. The Government hopes this should make intervention the exception rather than the rule.

7.49   The Government sees its proposal to require authorities to consult the Audit Commission or appropriate inspectorate on their action plans in the case of serious failure as reinforcing local accountability, and will make this a statutory requirement in the case of failures of substance. The Goverment wishes to establish a protocol with the LGA to ensure that the process of intervention is consistent with the framework for central-local relations which was agreed last year. This protocol will cover the specific circumstances where a fast track notification system is considered appropriate as well as the generality of cases.

7.50   Some individual Secretaries of State already have appropriate powers set out in statute for intervention in the local services for which they answer to Parliament. These arrangements will not be affected by the new general powers. The use of specific powers will be covered by any protocols agreed with the LGA but also appropriate to the nature and importance of the service at risk.

Police authorities

7.51   The duty to obtain best value will apply to police authorities. They will be required to act within the best value performance management framework (see Figure 7 above) securing year on year improvements in police services. The Government recognises that it would not be appropriate to expose to competition certain core statutory activities carried out by the police. Her Majesty's Inspector of Constabulary will undertake independent inspection within the best value framework. It will, like other inspectorates, continue to undertake other activities in support of Ministers alongside best value duties. Intervention powers will be available to Government to tackle serious or persistent failures in police services.

Timing and transitional arrangements

7.52   The duty of best value will be applied as quickly as possible after primary legislation is enacted. Although the Government will give further thought to the phasing of the specific provisions, it plans to require authorities to publish local performance plans early in the first financial year of best value. Local people will then have a baseline from which to consider their authority's current performance, and to contribute to the first of the reviews of performance which best value will require. Authorities are encouraged therefore to prepare for change now.

7.53   The Government confirms that it will introduce legislation to repeal the provisions that require CCT at the same time as the new duty of best value comes into force. It will throughout retain the capacity to act in the case of failure.

CHAPTER 8

Promoting the well-being of communities

- **Councils to promote economic, social and environmental well-being**

- **Vision and leadership for the whole community**

- **New partnership powers for councils**

- **New powers for pace-setting councils**

Community leadership

8.1 Community leadership is at the heart of the role of modern local government. Councils are the organisations best place to take a comprehensive overview of the needs and priorities of their local areas and communities and lead the work to meet those needs and priorities in the round.

8.2 Modern Britain faces a number of key challenges at the end of the twentieth century. Concerted action at local and national level is needed to address issues such as sustainable development, social exclusion, crime, education and training.

8.3 Councils are at the centre of local public service and local action to tackle these difficult issues. They have a wide range of diverse responsibilities which contribute to all aspects of their local communities, bring them into day to day contact with local people and which in many cases require them to work in partnership with others successfully.

8.4 So councils are ideally placed to work with government, their communities and the wide range of public, private and voluntary sector bodies who operate at local level and who need to come together if these challenges are to be successfully addressed. Local government has a long and proud tradition of developing innovative solutions to local problems.

8.5 In shaping policy in a number of areas, such as on education, public health, transport, the environment and the attack on crime and social exclusion, the Government has mapped out key roles for councils. In education, councils are being given a specific responsibility to promote high standards. They will be expected to work in partnership with self-managing schools to achieve this.

8.6 The Government is establishing key strategic partnerships between councils and the police, probation service and others to reduce crime and bring a more effective approach to youth justice, building on the key service responsibilities of local government. In deprived areas a combined approach – such as the New Deal for Communities – is the key to success. In public health and health care too, the Government is aiming to strengthen local partnerships – particularly between councils and the NHS – to tackle the social and economic causes of poor health and improve the delivery of health care and other related services. Councils will also be important parties, with the new Regional Development Agencies, in addressing the economic deficit in the English Regions.

8.7 The Government intends to ensure that councils are truly at the centre of public service locally, and that they are able to take the lead in developing a clear sense of direction for their communities and building partnerships to ensure the best for local communities.

A new duty to promote economic, social and environmental well-being

8.8 The Government intends to introduce legislation to place on councils a duty to promote the economic, social and environmental well-being of their areas and to strengthen councils' powers to enter into partnerships.

8.9 This new duty will provide an overarching framework for local government. It will enshrine in law the role of the council as the elected leader of their local community with a responsibility for the well-being and sustainable development of its area.

8.10 It will ensure that councils must, at all times, consider the long-term well-being of their area. It will put sustainable development at the heart of council decision making and will provide an overall framework within which councils must perform all their existing functions. So, in taking decisions affecting their area or its people, councils will have to weigh up the likely effects of a decision against the three objectives – economic, social and environmental – and if necessary strike a balance to ensure that the overall well-being of their area is achieved.

8.11 This new duty will be underpinned with a discretionary power enabling councils to take steps which in their view will promote the well-being of their area and those who live, work and visit there, providing that this is not used in ways which prejudice other council functions, or the functions of other statutory bodies. The Government will also retain a reserve power to exclude particular activities or to set a financial limit, where national interests might need to be protected.

Developing a strategy for the area – community planning

8.12 There is an overwhelming need for greater cohesion and coherence at the local level of all those – public sector, business, voluntary bodies – whose activities and efforts can affect local communities. The new duty to promote well-being will include a requirement for councils to secure the development of a comprehensive strategy for promoting the well-being of their area.

8.13 It is essential that there should be a clear and understandable strategy for every area, based on an analysis of the area's needs and priorities for future action. It should be developed with local people, local business and with public and voluntary sector bodies who operate in the local area.

8.14 The Government will not impose on councils any particular approach to this task – councils will have flexibility over the precise nature, scope and coverage of the strategy, the level of detailed action it contains and over how they go about preparing it in partnership with other organisations, with the new Regional Development Agencies which themselves will be preparing an economic strategy for their region, and with local people.

8.15 Many councils have made good progress in developing a Local Agenda 21 strategy for their area. This will complement the development of a strategy for promoting the well-being of the area. The LGA has also been instrumental in developing proposals, known as the 'New Commitment to Regeneration', which are now being piloted in 22 areas.

8.16 These strategies will increasingly form the backdrop to locally based bids for resources from central government and other sources such as the lottery distributors and regional development agencies. Councils will need to ensure that their other plans and strategies take into account the wider picture. These other plans will include their education development plans, their land use development plans, and their local transport plans as described in the White Paper – 'A New Deal for Transport: Better for Everyone'. Councils will need also to ensure coherence with local plans to which they contribute, but which are led by other agencies, for example Health Improvement Programmes.

Local scrutiny

8.17 A key element of community leadership is the responsibility that councils have to reflect local views and promote debate on issues of concern or relevance to local communities. Such issues can be wide ranging and may involve the roles and responsibilities of other institutions, business or private concerns.

Example 1 Community plan

Coventry City Council has initiated a process for all organisations in Coventry to agree on priorities and targets for the next five years to address the city's needs. The plan is organised around six priority areas: job creation, crime and community safety, tackling poverty, investing in young people, creating an exciting and vibrant city centre, and meeting the needs and aspirations of older people.

8.18   There are various ways in which this might be achieved. Some councils have established public forums to enable issues of particular local concern or interest to be aired and considered. Through this, people are able to air their views about matters which affect them, and other organisations and agencies are drawn more fully into the democratic debate, through their attendance at the public forum to explain their policies and actions.

8.19   The Government welcomes the steps taken by councils to convene local public forums. Although the Government does not wish to be prescriptive in the way that such forums might operate, one option may be for them to be organised on a similar basis to Parliamentary Select Committees. So, for example, backbench councillors with a particular interest might form a committee to take evidence in public and report on their findings, with recommendations where appropriate for the council or others.

8.20   The Government does not believe that it would be appropriate for these arrangements to alter the formal lines of accountability of other public bodies. Nor would it be right, or practical, to give councils powers to require participants to attend public forums or provide papers to forum members. Such steps could prove counterproductive, hindering the council's relationships with other local players, and would run contrary to the spirit of partnership and voluntary cooperation on which all effective relationships must be founded.

New powers to enter into partnerships

8.21   Effective local partnerships are fundamental to the success of councils' strategic role. It is essential that councils work with a wide range of agencies and organisations that operate locally, such as:

- local people, individually, and collectively through community groups, local women's organisations, and residents' associations;

- the local business community;

- voluntary groups (eg police liaison committees);

- private organisations (eg registered social landlords); and

- public bodies (eg executive agencies of Government, the new RDAs, TECs, and NHS bodies).

8.22   Although many councils have developed links with some of the bodies operating in their area, there is often a lack of cohesion between the various interest groups, and confusion over the powers of councils to participate with other stakeholders in partnership activities.

8.23   To remove this uncertainty, the Government intends to provide councils with clear discretionary powers to engage in partnership arrangements with other bodies, organisations or agencies that operate locally for any purpose which supports their functions, including the function of promoting the economic, social and environmental well-being of the area. The powers will provide scope for pooling or sharing of resources, accommodation, IT, staff, and will encourage the delegation of responsibility for decisions within an agreed framework or plan.

> ### Example 2 **Partnership project**
>
> The Thames Valley Partnership has been set up to improve community safety and reduce crime in the Thames Valley. It brings together local authorities, the police, Probation Service, and Prison Service, together with voluntary groups and local businesses. The Partnership works at a strategic level across the boundaries of different authorities to carry out research and disseminate good practice on a wide range of topics. Recent work has included early intervention to reduce criminality, and a range of youth projects and programmes to reduce specific types of crime – domestic violence, car crime, and retail crime.

8.24 This new power will help councils to establish joint arrangements with both statutory and non-statutory bodies and will clear up the current uncertainties about councils' powers to establish and participate in companies. With these powers, councils will be able to work with confidence with a whole range of other bodies to tackle difficult cross cutting issues.

Going further – a new framework

8.25 The Government recognises that the current statutory framework for councils can inhibit local innovation and diversity by setting out too rigidly the way in which particular functions must be discharged. It can get in the way of closer integration of council functions, such as social services, housing and education, to tackle social exclusion and improve service delivery. It can also limit the scope for working with other organisations.

8.26 The Government believes that there is scope to simplify the current framework for councils that can demonstrate that they have the ability and capacity to manage greater freedom and wider powers, and has set this as a longer term objective. In particular, the Government believes that beacon councils should be allowed greater scope to meet local needs and priorities.

8.27 The Government therefore intends to establish a statutory basis through which the best performing councils can be freed from some of the constraints which limit what they can do, and which stand in the way of improving service delivery to the public – including the provision of services which are the responsibility of other bodies.

8.28 The framework will also enable the Government and councils to try out alternative means of service delivery and to pilot new ideas, such as those emerging from departments in respect of action zones or from the Better Government project. Where councils come forward with new ideas and approaches of their own, the Government will respond positively, providing that the council concerned is running its affairs well and effectively, even if it is not a beacon council.

8.29 Such a framework would open the prospect for councils of increased responsibilities and greater opportunity to try out new ideas and to do more for the benefit of the local area and local people. The Government is clear that councils which perform consistently well will be able to acquire additional powers and freedoms that, over time, will be significantly wider than those available to councils which are performing less effectively.

8.30 These arrangements will provide an incentive for councils to modernise the way in which they work and improve their performance. Local people and local business will soon press for the improvements which would bring the performance of their council up to the standard necessary for greater local autonomy, and council leaders will quickly want to avail themselves of the wider scope for action which certain other councils will have.

CHAPTER 9

Capital finance

- **Investment for modernisation**

- **A simpler system for capital investment**

- **Better long term planning**

- **Incentives for better asset management**

- **Easier PFI and partnerships**

9.1   Education, health, transport, and housing infrastructure – in which local government is vitally important– need to be renewed if we are to modernise this country and improve people's quality of life.

9.2   On 11 June the Chancellor announced in his statement on the Economic and Fiscal Strategy a near doubling of net public sector investment over the next three years. The Comprehensive Spending Review[13] includes substantive proposals to meet this target. Spending on schools will double over the course of this Parliament. There will be an additional £3.6 billion from capital receipts to reduce the backlog of repairs to council houses, and £700 million more for local authority transport capital to establish 150 new local transport plans and to restore cuts in the maintenance of principal roads. The New Deal for Regeneration will tackle the problems of the most deprived areas, through the allocation of £800 million for the New Deal for Communities, and £2.3 billion through a re-shaped Single Regeneration Budget. This new money is conditional on modernisation, the implementation of reform, and setting and meeting clear targets for modern, efficient and effective services.

9.3   In addition, the Treasury will administer a Capital Modernisation Fund (CMF) of £2.5 billion. Government Departments will be able to take into account local authority projects in preparing bids for this. The CMF will be allocated on a competitive basis, to provide resources for innovative capital or Private Finance Initiative (PFI) projects which improve key services or public infrastructure.

13 House of Commons Official Report: Vol 316, No. 206, Col 187, 14 July 1998.

9.4 Councils have a large role to play in addressing the backlog of public sector investment, and the Government recognises the need to provide councils with the means to play their role effectively. Accordingly, the Government will modernise the capital finance framework for councils, so that it is both simpler and more readily understandable. The framework will strongly encourage councils to spend the provision available for capital in the most effective manner, and to review rigorously their existing asset holdings. The Government will also consider how to provide more freedom for capital investment in developing services by councils who have qualified for beacon status in those services.

9.5 The capital finance framework covers both procedures for allocating capital investment resources to councils, and a system of rules and regulations governing how they can use these. The Government proposes a long-term framework for investment, by:

- improving the allocation procedures, to enable councils to use their investment resources to get the best results;

- introducing greater certainty and stability over levels of resources, to improve long-term planning and increase value for money;

- encouraging councils to manage their assets to the best effect;

- developing the role of local authority companies and the PFI;

- allowing greater freedom for the best authorities; and

- examining alternative arrangements for regulating capital finance in the longer-term.

A single capital pot

9.6 At present, a number of separate service-specific funding mechanisms are used to allocate capital resources to councils. The trend over recent years has been an increasing use of allocations for restricted purposes and a consequent reduction in block allocations that can be used flexibly to meet a range of spending priorities.

9.7 The Government will introduce a cross-service allocation for the bulk of central government capital support to councils – a single capital pot. This approach offers benefits in terms of increased local accountability and autonomy, stability of allocations, and flexibility. It will allow councils to take greater responsibility for the internal allocation of their resources among services and a greater opportunity to address cross-cutting issues such as social exclusion effectively.

9.8 The Government recognises that the creation of a single capital pot would be a step change that could not be implemented overnight. It would for example require the development of a cross-service needs indicator. In addition, it is important that the strengths of existing allocation arrangements and the Government's overall policy priorities are not jeopardised. For example, improving the infrastructure of the nation's schools through the New Deal for Schools is crucial to the the successful implementation of the School Standards and Framework Bill.

9.9 The Government will incorporate specific safeguards so as to ensure, for example, that schools' capital is allocated in a way which will guarantee delivery of the Government's objectives. As previously indicated, it might not be appropriate for allocations for specialised and geographically dispersed projects – such as for coastal protection and flood defence – to be included in the single pot. The Government will consult the LGA and others on the timing and details of implementation. The single pot will not be implemented before the financial year 2001/02.

9.10 Resources from the single pot would be allocated partly according to a needs based formula and partly by competitive assessment of councils' service and corporate capital strategies, and of their performance in delivering them. The needs based formula used in making allocations would be intended to encompass all services, but would reflect important priorities in particular services. The resulting allocation would reflect an aggregate of capital needs in all services.

9.11 Competitive assessment would be based around a comprehensive capital strategy, linked to service strategies, in line with the principles of best value. An authority's capital strategy would be expected to address:

- value and condition of assets

- priorities and plans for local area and partners

- capital implications of service delivery plans (as part of Local Performance Plans – required under best value)

- community needs and service priorities

- key government policy objectives

- funding opportunities (including linkages with the New Deal for Regeneration, European Union funds, the National Lottery, and Public/Private Partnerships)

- revenue implications of investment decisions

- needs and contribution from business

- accountability to the community.

9.12 The Government would base assessments of performance on indicators of good practice and other accepted benchmarks, as well as on councils' achievements of their own performance targets. Such factors would both inform, and be informed by, the assessment of best value within councils.

9.13 There would also need to be safeguards for communities in those few cases where it was felt that the council needed to make significant improvements to their decision-making and project evaluation procedures. In these circumstances resources could temporarily be allocated on a service specific basis in some or all service areas until the authority could benefit from the single pot approach.

9.14   In the intervening period before the introduction of the single pot the Government believes that significant improvements are possible. Ways will be found to increase local choice and encourage the development of corporate and strategic thinking in authorities, the use of private finance, and partnership with the local community and business. Examples include the proposals for a single pot for housing from 2000/01, on which the Government will be consulting.

Greater certainty in resource allocation

9.15   The introduction of the single capital pot, coupled with the move to the new public expenditure regime, will help to provide the greater long-term stability over resources that is essential, if councils are to deliver their capital strategies effectively. The total levels of central government support will be set out in three-year plans, and the use of simple and stable needs formulae will increase the predictability of allocations to individual councils. The extended planning horizon will allow councils to take a more strategic, long-term view of their capital programmes, ensuring greater effectiveness in the use of capital resources and better value for money for the public purse.

9.16   Some capital resources, in particular those relating to large individual projects – such as major road schemes – or to the achievement of very specific government programmes, are likely to continue to be allocated as specific funding, rather than through the single pot. The ability to make effective use of specific allocations will be improved by the increased end year flexibility now permitted to Departments on capital and by the issue of such allocations in the form of supplementary credit approvals for periods of up to two years, increasing their flexibility and removing the perverse incentive to rush expenditure at year end.

Encouraging best practice in asset management: abolition of non-housing set-aside

9.17   The Government is committed to making the most of existing public assets. For example, we have commissioned research into the practical issues that may arise from local authorities and other public sector bodies sharing accommodation and thus economising on costs overall. The Government has also announced a new *Invest to Save* budget to encourage different parts of the public sector to work together in innovative ways through, for example, one stop shops, electronic service delivery and single-site offices. Initiatives of this kind will continue.

9.18   Demanding but achievable targets are being set for the sale of local government assets. To increase the incentive for councils to raise receipts and to encourage greater local investment the Government has announced its intention to abolish, with effect from 1 September, the existing requirement to set aside for debt repayment part of the money received from selling capital assets, other than housing and related land. The change is subject to parliamentary approval and will be introduced after a brief period of consultation with councils. The controls will, however, remain in place for housing and related assets, and for certain special cases. The change will simplify the operation of the capital finance system and provide authorities with greater freedom to spend their resources as they wish.

9.19   It is vital to develop better performance indicators and benchmarks for property management, so that best practice in asset management can be identified and rewarded. Such indicators will form an essential element of Asset Management Plans and will contribute to the assessment of best value. Such plans broadly comprise strategies intended to achieve more effective use of assets. They can help managers to prioritise and set maintenance programmes, and to predict the pattern of future maintenance needs. They should let managers identify inefficient assets, and help them secure a better (not necessarily financial) return on investments. The Government will commission further research into asset management, and will consult with the LGA and professional bodies on the issues raised.

Distribution of resources to reflect capital receipts

9.20　The system for distributing resources to councils for capital investment will be demonstrably fairer if it continues to take some account of resources available locally through the sale of property and other assets ('capital receipts'). Such a system allows the Government to target resources on those areas of greatest need within a fixed total of public spending. While a number of concerns have been raised by councils about the method currently used to take account of capital receipts (the RTIA system), a clear consensus has not emerged in favour of any of the options outlined in the consultation paper, or of any alternative means of redistribution. Given the lack of a clear preference for change, the Government intends to keep the system under review as part of the process of developing the single pot.

Local authority companies

9.21　The Government announced to Parliament on 11 June a relaxation of the controls over borrowing and investment by local authority airport companies. Airport companies whose finances are sufficiently sound will be allowed to borrow to finance airport related investment in the UK, where the lending would be genuinely commercial.

9.22　The Government will consider further how these controls apply to various categories of local authority company, including the question of the boundary between local authority companies whose investment is subject to the capital finance rules, and those which fall outside the regulatory framework.

Private finance initiative

9.23　The Government regards the development of the PFI for local authorities as a high priority, as demonstrated by the further substantial increase in support for it announced in the CSR. The PFI is an important option within the process of seeking best value in the delivery of local authority services. The Government will seek to ensure that councils consider all their options on service delivery, including PFI, in a way which avoids distortions in decision making and maximises overall value for money.

Greater freedom for the best councils

9.24　The concept of beacon councils, who can be relied upon to conduct their affairs prudently and responsibly in regard to some or all of their services and hence can be given significant additional freedoms and powers, has been described in Chapter 2. They could be given more freedom to make their own decisions on the amount of capital expenditure they could afford on the services where they are recognized as having beacon status. One way of doing this within the existing capital finance system would be to issue them with additional supplementary credit approvals for capital investment in those services. These credit approvals would not be accompanied by any increase in revenue support for debt servicing costs; authorities receiving them would need to consider carefully the extent to which they could finance additional expenditure and consequent borrowing within their revenue budgets, and exercise judgement accordingly in the extent to which they used these approvals. The Government will consider further the detailed arrangements for providing additional capital freedoms, within the framework of public expenditure control, and consult on them as part of the overall process of consultation on the establishment of a scheme for beacon councils.

Longer-term options for regulating capital finance

9.25 The Government will continue to keep the capital finance system under review and work will be commissioned to examine the practicalities of alternative arrangements such as the concept of debt/revenue ratios proposed by the LGA. (In broad terms, the proposal is that councils should be free to borrow subject only to prudential accounting limits that would relate the level of debts and other liabilities that they could incur to their future revenue income). This work will include further consideration of the possible replacement of Minimum Revenue Provision – the statutory rule designed to ensure that councils make provision to repay debt and meet other credit liabilities – with a less formal but prudentially sound scheme of provision for debt repayment.

CHAPTER 10

Business rates

- **National business rates to be retained**

- **Partnerships with local businesses to plan local spending**

- **Limited local rates**

A local rate

THE NEED FOR PARTNERSHIP

10.1   The actions of councils are vital to the competitiveness of local business. Business performance is affected by local education standards, the crime rate and the opportunities available locally to employees for child care and services for elderly relatives. Councils' regeneration strategies and transport and planning policies can be crucial to the success of local business.

10.2   It is vital therefore that the links between local businesses and councils are strong and effective. Business, community leaders and local people need to work together to improve the delivery of existing services, and to determine local priorities and spending programmes.

10.3   This chapter sets out a broad framework for a reformed business rate system which would strengthen the relationship between councils and their local businesses. The Government will consult further with local government, business and others about the details of implementation.

SETTING RATES LOCALLY

10.4 An atmosphere of trust between councils and local business requires regular, open dialogue, where both parties recognise their mutual interests and work together in partnership. Allowing some measure of local discretion over the business rate would help to achieve this.

10.5 If councils have some direct responsibility for local tax decisions affecting the business community, their local leadership role would be enhanced. They would be more responsive to business needs. Local business would have a greater claim on the attention of councils and a greater interest in helping to develop a vision for the better delivery of local services and the improvement of the local area.

10.6 Before allowing councils a measure of discretion over local business rates, there must be effective arrangements for the involvement of business in local tax and spending decisions, and greater efforts by local authorities to build constructive partnerships with local firms. Any system of local rates must also provide adequate safeguards against unreasonable rate increases and must, so far as possible, be stable, predictable, and comprehensible.

10.7 The present system of national non-domestic rates has considerable strengths. It is a readily comprehensible tax which is stable and predictable. It provides a level playing field across the country. The rating pool protects business and councils from the impact of changes in the local tax base, which would otherwise result in higher local taxes or poorer services. The system, along with the Revenue Support Grant arrangements, provides a degree of resource equalisation, without which councils would have to set widely different local tax levels to provide a similar level of service, given the uneven distribution of rateable resources across the country.

10.8 The Government therefore intends:

- to retain a national non-domestic rate which will be set annually by the Government; the revenue from the rate will be paid into a non-domestic rating pool and redistributed to councils, much as now;

- that councils should agree arrangements with their local business community to involve business in their expenditure planning and to build effective partnerships with business rate payers;

- to consult on the details of a scheme to allow councils, within centrally prescribed limits, to set a supplementary local rate, or to give a rebate on the national rate; any supplementary rate would help finance additional discretionary spending on priorities agreed with business and the local community (see Figure 9);

- at the same time as introducing any such local rate scheme to consider changing the rating system to reduce the rates bills of small businesses.

Figure 9 How a local rate scheme might work

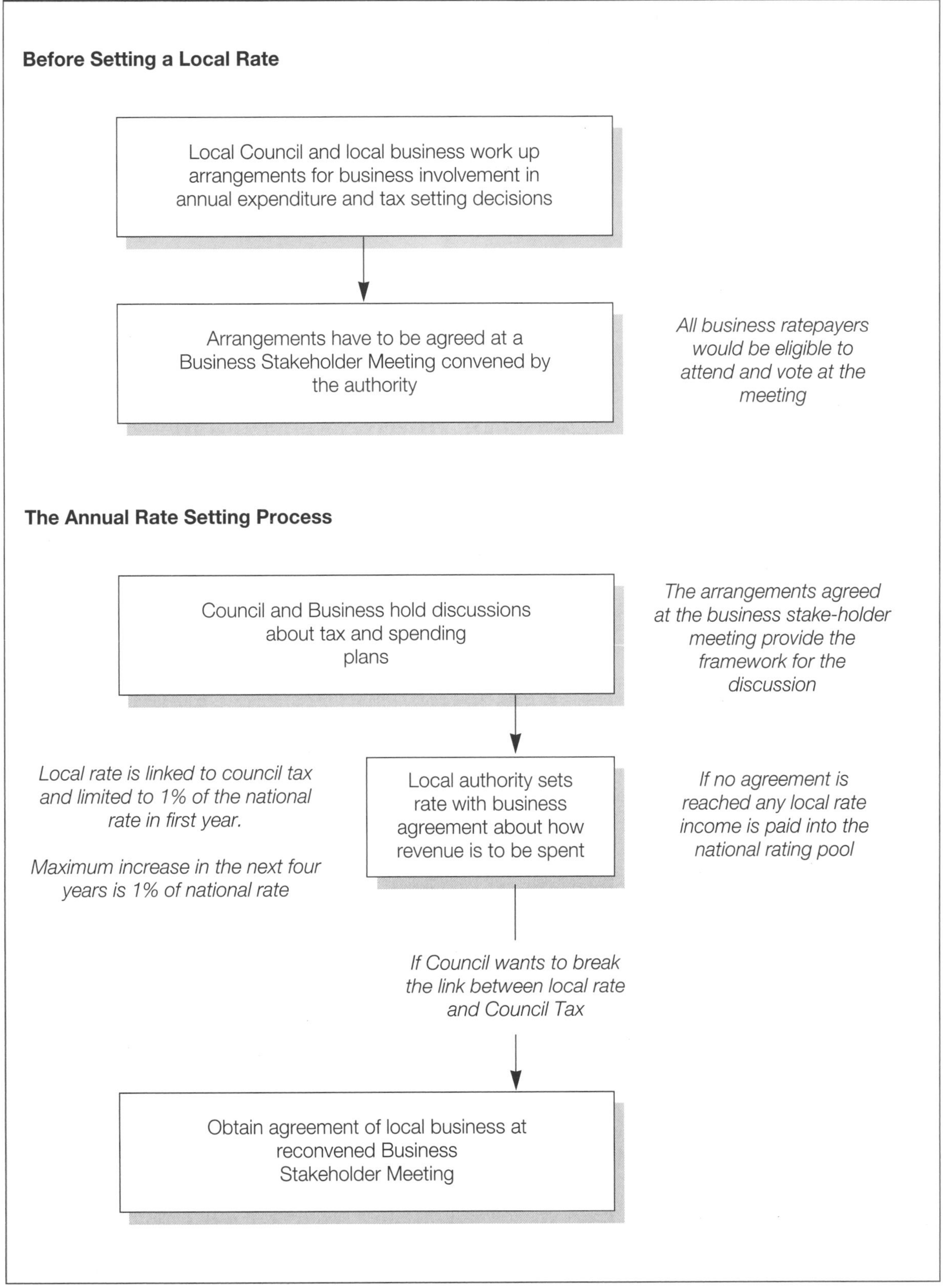

Before Setting a Local Rate

Local Council and local business work up arrangements for business involvement in annual expenditure and tax setting decisions

Arrangements have to be agreed at a Business Stakeholder Meeting convened by the authority

All business ratepayers would be eligible to attend and vote at the meeting

The Annual Rate Setting Process

Council and Business hold discussions about tax and spending plans

The arrangements agreed at the business stake-holder meeting provide the framework for the discussion

Local rate is linked to council tax and limited to 1% of the national rate in first year.

Maximum increase in the next four years is 1% of national rate

Local authority sets rate with business agreement about how revenue is to be spent

If no agreement is reached any local rate income is paid into the national rating pool

If Council wants to break the link between local rate and Council Tax

Obtain agreement of local business at reconvened Business Stakeholder Meeting

INVOLVEMENT OF BUSINESS IN THE LOCAL RATE

10.9 In advance of any legislation to implement such a scheme, the Government would expect councils to ensure that they have effective arrangements in place to involve local business in tax and spending decisions.

10.10 Councils should work with local business to establish partnership arrangements and involve the business community in their strategic planning, tax and spending decisions. The arrangements might differ from one authority to another depending on local circumstances. They should not be limited to spending and local tax decisions, but should encompass the full range of matters in which business has an interest, for example, in community and local performance plans.

10.11 The Government expects councils to get the broad agreement of local business to the arrangements, through a 'Business Stakeholder Meeting', to which the council would invite all their business ratepayers. Businesses unable to attend might be encouraged to register proxy votes.

10.12 In legislating for local rates, the Government would need to take reserve powers to impose arrangements on local communities where such arrangements had not been established and where the agreement of either party was being unreasonably withheld.

THE USE OF LOCAL RATE INCOME

10.13 Once agreed, the arrangements would govern the way in which local rate decisions are taken. As part of these arrangements councils would have to agree with their local business community how any local rate income was to be used, but business ratepayers would not be allowed to block the setting of a local rate.

10.14 The Government would also need to ensure that the local rate system contained adequate mechanisms to resolve the situation where councils and the local business community could not reach any agreement on the use of the income from the supplementary rate. The Government suggests that in these circumstances the local rate would have to be paid by local businesses, but the council would have to pay the income into the Pool, from where it would be redistributed to all councils in the normal way. This arrangement would provide an incentive to both parties – local businesses and the council – to reach agreement.

THE CENTRAL LIMITS

10.15 In order that councils could not introduce unreasonably large local rates and to ensure that business had some certainty about the level of future rate bills, the local rate would be constrained by a central limit set by the Government .

10.16 To introduce local rates without undue turbulence, and to preserve the stability and predictability of the current arrangements, the Government intends that the limit should be set so that councils could not increase the annual rate by more than 1% of the national rate in any one year, up to a maximum, over time, of 5%.

A LINK WITH COUNCIL TAX

10.17   So that business could not be asked to bear a disproportionate share of any local expenditure, there would also need to be a relationship between the supplementary local rate and council taxes. The Government will continue to consult about how this might best be formulated.

ADJUSTING THE LINK

10.18   There may be circumstances in which councils, with the agreement of their local businesses, might want to adjust the link with council tax and raise a local rate, up to the central limit, for spending on locally agreed priorities.

10.19   In such cases, they could be allowed to do so, but only where they had obtained the agreement of local business ratepayers, perhaps at a specially convened Business Stakeholder Meeting. If that agreement was not forthcoming, the council would not be permitted to vary the rate in this way.

BEACON COUNCILS

10.20   The Government might also allow overall beacon councils greater freedom to set local business rates.

10.21   This would ensure that extra resources could be raised locally and directed at locally agreed priorities, but only in those areas where the council had shown that it was capable of making the most effective use of them.

10.22   Where a council had secured beacon status, and had demonstrated that it had an effective working relationship with its local business community, that council might be permitted to set an additional local rate.

10.23   The additional local rate would be limited to a further 1% of the national rate in any one year, up to a further 5% maximum.

10.24   In order to give communities sufficient flexibility to respond to local circumstances, the Government will consider allowing beacon councils to levy the additional local rate across the whole of their area, just part of it, or on specific classes of business ratepayer, providing that councils secure the agreement of the affected ratepayers.

10.25   This additional source of local rate income need not be subject to a statutory link with council tax. Instead, it, and the expenditure which it was intended to finance, could be determined as part of the arrangements for consultation and involvement worked out between the council and its local business community.

10.26   As for the main local rate, the Government would need to ensure that there were mechanisms to resolve situations where councils and local business were unable to agree on the use of the income.

SMALL BUSINESSES

10.27   There is evidence to suggest that the rates, as a proportion of turnover and profits, are greater for small businesses than for large. Research commissioned by the Department in 1995 found that companies with a turnover of less than £100,000 per year paid over 30% of their operating profits in rates – twice as much as larger companies and ten times as much as the very biggest companies with an annual turnover of £1 billion, or more.

10.28   The research findings are supported by the responses of small firms to the consultation paper, which highlighted the disproportionate rate burden faced by small businesses.

10.29   Such evidence as there is, supports the view that small businesses occupy properties with lower rateable values – predominantly those in the £0 – £5,000 range. When the Government introduces local rates it will consider introducing measures to reduce the rating burden on small businesses.

10.30   The Government will discuss the details of any scheme with business representatives, and others, but we intend that it should be targeted at properties with rateable values below £5,000 and that its cost should be met through a modest increase in the national multiplier of about 1p – or less than 2%.

POSTSCRIPT
Making it happen

This White Paper has mapped out an agenda for the reform and modernisation of English local government. An agenda focused on a bigger say and a better deal for local people. The Government is committed to it. Its success will be assured as councils everywhere join in partnership with the Government to bring about a fundamental shift in power and influence in favour of local people.

This is not an agenda for the next year or two, but for change stretching for ten years or more – well into the 21st century. Some changes are already underway, some can be started now, and others will need more time before they can begin.

The Government has begun to play its part to motivate and encourage change. It now looks to the LGA and others to join with it to take forward this vital work. And it will as Parliamentary time allows seek the legislation necessary for councils to change and modernise fully.

Some councils have already made a start. As this Paper has demonstrated, councils everywhere can now begin actively to develop new political structures, improve local democracy, build up their role as community leaders, and to secure best value in service delivery. They should not wait for legislation before considering how to make further progress.

As legislation is enacted, further opportunities will open for councils. Councils will need to seize them, and to use them imaginatively if they are to give the best to their local people.

This agenda gives councils the opportunity once again to be a force for progress and social justice in their local communities. It presents a future where the partnership between Government, councils and the people makes a real difference to everyone's quality of life.

ANNEX

The Chronology of Change: Key Dates in English Local Government History

1834: **Poor Law Amendment Act**
begins succession of legislation changing the shape and structure of local administration by setting up Boards of Guardians as special purpose parish authorities.

1835: **Municipal Corporations Act**
establishes directly elected corporate boroughs in place of the self-electing medieval corporations which had become widely discredited and often corrupt.

1888: **Local Government Act**
establishes 62 Elected County Councils, including the London County Council, and 61 all-purpose County Borough Councils in England and Wales.

1894: **Local Government Act**
revives parish councils and establishes 535 Urban District Councils, 472 Rural District Councils and 270 non-county Borough Councils.

1899: **London Government Act**
sets up 28 Metropolitan Borough Councils in London and the Corporation of London.

1925: **Royal Commission on Local Government**
reports for the first time, under the chairmanship of the Earl of Onslow, with a further report published in 1929.

1929: **Local Government Act**
abolishes the Poor Law Guardians Boards and transfers functions to local government.

1963: **London Government Act**
creates 32 London Boroughs and a Greater London Council (GLC).

1966: **Royal Commission on Local Government in England**
is established under the chairmanship of Lord Redcliffe-Maud, reports in 1969.

1970: **Reform of Local Government in England White Paper**
supports most of the findings of the Royal Commission, particularly in respect of unitary local government.

1971: **Local Government in England White Paper**
rejects unitary authorities and supports two-tier local government throughout England and Wales.

1972: **Local Government Act**
removes Country Borough Councils, reduces the number of County Councils in England and Wales to 47, establishes 6 Metropolitan County Councils and 36 Metropolitan District Councils.

1980: Local Government Planning and Land Act
establishes Compulsory Competitive Tendering and Urban Development Corporations.

1983: Streamlining the Cities White Paper
proposes to abolish the GLC and 6 Metropolitan County Councils and replace them with joint boards and ad hoc agencies.

1984: Rates Act
establishes system of rate-capping.

1985: Local Government Act
abolishes the GLC and the 6 Metropolitan County Councils and establishes a directly-elected Inner London Education Authority(ILEA), 24 centrally appointed bodies and 16 London-wide local government bodies.

1986: Committee of Inquiry into the Conduct of Local Authority Business
chaired by David Widdecombe, reports on political organisation of local government.

1988: Local Government Finance Act
replaces domestic rates with the Community Charge or "Poll Tax".

1988: Education Reform Act
abolishes the Inner London Education Authority.

1989: Local Government and Housing Act
implements the Widdecombe report on political organisation and establishes basis of present capital finance system.

1992: Local Government Finance Act
replaces "Poll Tax" with Council Tax.

1992: Local Government Act
supports further structural reorganisation to create some new unitary councils.

1996: Select Committee on Relations Between Central and Local Government
chaired by Lord Hunt of Tanworth, publishes its report, "Rebuilding Trust", supporting change and experimentation in political organisation.

1997: Local Government and Rating Act
supports new opportunities for parish council formation and protection for village shops.

1997: Local Government Finance (Supplementary Credit Approvals) Act
provides basis for release of capital receipts.

1997: Local Government (Contracts) Act
confirms authorities' powers to enter into contracts.

1998: A Mayor and Assembly for London White Paper
proposed establishment of Greater London Assembly with a separate directly-elected mayor for London, subsequently receives overwhelming support in referendum.

1998: Modern Local Government: In Touch with the People White Paper

Acknowledgements:
Page 12: Children playing - courtesy of Reading Borough Council
Page 17: Man and woman at computer - courtesy of Gosport Borough Council
Page 19: School assembly - courtesy of John Birdsall Photography
Page 23: Woman at bus stop - courtesy of Guzelian
Page 24: Council chamber - courtesy of Lewisham Borough Council/David Allen@ Waymark
Page 41: Supermarket voting – courtesy of the Municipal Journal
Page 47: Council tax office – courtesy of Redcar and Cleveland Borough Council
Page 49: Meeting – courtesy of Redcar and Cleveland Borough Council
Page 63: Young girl – courtesy of John Birdsall Photography
Page 64: Street cleaner – courtesy of London Borough of Newham
Page 77: Police with child – courtesy of Cleveland Police
Page 79: Gardener – courtesy of Oldham Metropolitan Borough Council
Page 87: Building site – courtesy of Gosport Borough Council
Page 91: People in street – courtesy of Ipswich Borough Council
Page 97: Two women laughing – John Birdsall Photography